# *More* **Embroidery Machine ESSENTIALS**

## How to Customize, Edit, and Create Decorative Designs

## By Jeanine Twigg

Published by

 **krause publications**
An F&W Publications Company

**700 East State Street • Iola, WI 54990-0001**
**715-445-2214 • 888-457-2873**
**www.krause.com**

Please call or write for our free catalog of publications. Our toll-free number, to place an order or to obtain a free catalog, is 800-258-0929. Please use our regular business telephone 715-445-2214 for editorial comment and further information.

Library of Congress Catalog Number 2003101327
ISBN 0-87349-439-3

The following terms are trademarked/registered: Windows®, Macintosh®, and Zip®

## Copyright Information for the CD-ROM:

# Table of Contents

*Mixed-media wall hanging by Cindy Losekamp.*

## Chapter 3 —
## Introduction to Software . . .26

*Stand-alone dimensional embroidery design by Linda McGehee.*

## Chapter 4 —
## Customizing, Stitch Editing, and Resizing . . . . . . . . . . . . .40

*Another stand-alone design from Linda McGehee.*

# Acknowledgments

## Product Manufacturers

This book would not be possible without the generosity of the following companies whose contribution of equipment, software, supplies, designs, and more fill the pages of this book. As an author and embroidery consumer, I cannot thank you enough for sharing your wonderful products for inclusion in this book.

| | |
|---|---|
| Amazing Designs | Hobbyware |
| Baby Lock | Hoop-It-All |
| Bernina | Husqvarna Viking |
| Bo-Nash | Janome |
| Brother | JT Trading |
| Bubble's Menagerie | OESD |
| BuzzTools | Pfaff |
| Cactus Punch | Sew Artfully Yours |
| Dakota Collectibles | Singer |
| Elna | Sulky |
| Embroideryarts | Sullivans |
| Em-Grid | Superior Threads |
| Gingher | YLI |

## Designers

The Inspirational Embroidery Showcase would not be possible without the contributions from the following designers. Your talent and creativity amaze me!

| | |
|---|---|
| Annette Bailcy | Richards Jarden |
| Mac Berg | Linda Griepentrog |
| Bernina Sewing | Jody Hooker |
| Center of Michigan | Cindy Losekamp |
| Nicky Bookout | Linda McGehee |
| Dana Botranger | Mary Mulari |
| Nancy Cornwell | Penny Muncaster-Jewell |
| Robert Decker | Sulky of America |
| Elna Educators | Vermillion Stitchery |
| Janome Educators | Nancy Zieman |

### A NOTE FROM JEANINE:

In addition, I'd like to thank Melinda Bylow for the awesome illustrations, fashion drawings, and layout of this book; Craig Dunmore for the digitizing of the designs; and my family, friends, and colleagues for their patience and understanding during the coordination of this book and the entire *Embroidery Machine Essentials* series.

## Industry Experts

The following industry experts have contributed embroidery hints and tips throughout the pages of this book. You can identify their quotes within colorful text boxes like this:

> I love to think outside the box for my embroidery adventures. My biggest question is "What if I did...?" as I think of what to try next—whether it's embroidering on metal or trying a new design in a nontraditional way.
>
> **– Linda Griepentrog**

**Annette Bailey**, editor of *Creative Machine Embroidery* magazine

**Mac Berg**, freelance educator and owner of the Lakeshore Sewing Depot in Waukegan, Ill.

**Nicky Bookout**, freelance educator and designer

**Melinda Bylow**, freelance art director and graphic artist

**Regena Carlevaro**, merchandise supervisor, Janome America

**Bonnie Colonna**, freelance educator for Husqvarna Viking

**Robert Decker**, freelance educator for Husqvarna Viking and owner of the Decker Design Studio

**Donna Vermillion Giampa**, owner of The Vermillion Stitchery

**Linda Griepentrog**, editor of *Sew News* magazine and editorial director of *Creative Machine Embroidery* magazine

**Richards Jarden,** owner of Embroideryarts

**Penny Muncaster-Jewell**, freelance educator and author of several books including *Penny's Practical Guide to PE-Design, Palette,* and *Deco Wizard* series, and the *Not Just Another Fish on a T-Shirt* book

**Lisa Shaw**, author of several BuzzTools CD-ROM tutorials, technical support manager for BuzzTools, and owner of Bubble's Menagerie

**Nancy Zieman**, president of Nancy's Notions, host of *Sewing With Nancy* on PBS, and author of numerous sewing books

# Introduction

As I was helping my oldest daughter with a science project recently, I realized that the testing and analyzing that goes into a science experiment is a lot like embroidery. Consider the embroidery process one large science project. Test stitching designs and analyzing results is all part of an embroidery experiment. We have many choices of fabrics, designs, threads, needles, and stabilizers that no two combinations end with the same results. In this next step of the embroidery process, it will be important to continue experimenting while customizing, editing, and creating decorative designs in order to achieve successful results.

*More Embroidery Machine Essentials* is designed as a basic reference guide for use with all brands of embroidery equipment and software. In addition to this book, read the embroidery machine and software owner's manuals, take classes from the dealer that honors your equipment warranties, and view software "Help" menus, videos, and tutorials to gain more knowledge. There are plenty of helpful reference guides available to answer questions as you continue through your embroidery adventure.

The touch-screen of an embroidery machine may have design customizing, editing, and digitizing features. However, these functions are limited compared to the capabilities of embroidery software. If your embroidery machine does not have the design modification functions you desire, then consider using embroidery software to enhance your capabilities.

Only after you feel confident using an embroidery machine should you move on to the use of software. In order to make your experience with software successful, you **must** have the ability to fall back on your embroidery machine experience to analyze problems.

The 10 embroidery designs and graphic images on the CD-ROM have been produced exclusively for this book—you cannot get them anywhere else. Each design can be used to experiment with a multitude of embroidery software techniques. The designs are available in home and commercial embroidery machine formats, and are accompanied by the original graphic images in several popular file formats to experiment in digitizing software.

*A NOTE FROM JEANINE:*

People run computers… computers do not run people. Remember that you have control of the computer!

Be patient—there is a learning curve when using embroidery software. Some people are more computer literate and learn fast, while others, with no computer experience, need a little extra time to learn the process. Give yourself time to adjust and be sure to take classes to help you through the process.

By the time you're finished reading this book from cover to cover, you'll have a better understanding of the next step in the embroidery process. Have fun and be sure to keep *Embroidery Machine Essentials* and *More Embroidery Machine Essentials* by your side every step of the way!

Your embroidery friend,

*Jeanine*

## Jeanine's Quilt

The front cover quilt features a raggedy edge finish with embroidered outline quilt designs to hold the individual layers together. There are a variety of books available that feature projects with the raggedy edge finish. Choose a favorite outline motif and quilt pattern, or use a basic 6" square block as shown.

To embroider the fabric, cut 6" squares from three layers of unwashed flannel for each square. Flip the back square rightside out. Flannel does not shift, so the embroidery process is a snap.

For best results, hoop a layer of water-soluble mesh, spray the stabilizer with temporary adhesive, center the first 6" flannel layer in the hoop, and embroider the design with a cotton variegated thread. Use a perimeter basting stitch to hold the layers together if available for your equipment. Trim the stabilizer within 1/2" of the embroidery. Repeat for the remaining blocks.

Once the embroidery process is complete, start the block assembly process. Use a 1/2" seam allowance to sew the blocks with backsides together.

After the quilt is assembled, snip the raw edge seam allowances perpendicular to the seamline. Cut within 1/8" of the seamline. For best results, use an electric scissors by folding the quilt backsides together at each raw edge and cut the seam allowance between 3/8" and 1/2" increments.

After the seam allowance trimming, wash the quilt in warm water and tumble dry on a medium height. Clean the dryer lint trap often as a lot of lint is collected.

The process is complete when the seam allowances have blossomed, and there is a huge grin on your face!

# Chapter 1
# *More* Embroidery Essentials

This book is a continuation of *Embroidery Machine Essentials,* which provides the basics of how to hoop, stabilize, and stitch decorative designs. The next step in the embroidery process is to customize, edit, and create decorative designs using an embroidery machine or accompanying software.

For successful results, it is important to master the use of an embroidery machine before starting the next step. Start slowly and work your way into the use of embroidery software. Most importantly, become friends with your embroidery equipment!

*More Embroidery Machine Essentials* provides the basics to you get started. The CD-ROM inside the back cover contains the following files that will help you along the way.

- A comprehensive glossary of terms in PDF (Portable Document Format) files

- An Inches-to-Millimeters Conversion Chart for use in embroidery software

- 10 Exclusive Embroidery Designs in appropriate embroidery machine file formats

- Design Details in a PDF file

- Graphic Images in BMP and WMF file formats for use in digitizing software

- Adobe Acrobat 5.01 software in Windows® and Macintosh® versions for use to view the PDF files

---

***IMPORTANT NOTE:***

The computer information and instructions in this book are for use with Windows-based operating systems. Those using Macintosh-based operating systems can use this book, but know that the keyboard or basic computer operating features may be slightly different in appearance and function. If possible, use software that can simulate the use of a Windows-based operating system.

---

## *More* Exclusive Embroidery Designs

The 10 exclusive embroidery designs are used throughout the pages that follow to show you how to customize, edit, and create decorative designs. To access the designs, insert the CD-ROM into your computer. The designs are located in folders for each embroidery machine format. Copy the design files to your computer. Be sure to copy only the design format compatible with your brand of embroidery equipment.

### Design Details

The Design Details found on the CD-ROM provide the design segment and thread color change information. Use these pages as a guide during the embroidery process. Each time the embroidery machine stops, it is considered the end of a segment. It may not require a thread color change.

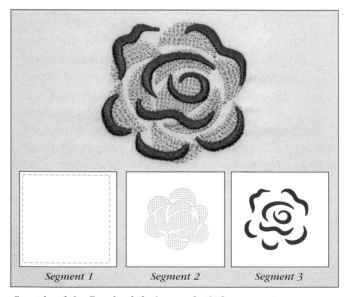

| Segment 1 | Segment 2 | Segment 3 |

*Sample of the Rosebud design and stitch segments.*

The exact thread color numbers are not included. Choose thread colors based on the your personal preference and the project fabric color.

### Perimeter Baste

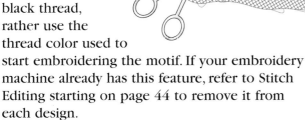

Each design includes a perimeter basting stitch to hold the fabric and stabilizer layers together during the embroidery process. The first thread color in each design is black and represents the perimeter baste. It is not necessary to use black thread, rather use the thread color used to start embroidering the motif. If your embroidery machine already has this feature, refer to Stitch Editing starting on page 44 to remove it from each design.

The perimeter baste is quick and easy to remove after the embroidery process. On the stabilizer side of the fabric, snip the bobbin threads every three to four stitches. Then, turn to the fabric right side to pull up on the long top thread to remove the stitches. The bobbin threads will poke up on top of the fabric and are easy to remove.

### Copyright Laws

The designs and accompanying graphic images are copyrighted. You can use the designs for your personal embroidery projects or for embroidered items for sale. It is illegal to share, trade, copy, sell, or distribute these designs. For more information on the copyright laws that govern embroidery designs, visit **www.embroideryprotection.com** on the Internet. Respect of the copyright laws protects the designers and thereby assures a steady supply of original designs with high quality digitizing and standards.

---

## More Embroidery Products

Manufacturers of embroidery products are continuously developing new ways to make embroidery more fun and creative. From hardware to software, embroidery is one of the fastest growing segments of the sewing industry. Visit your local embroidery machine dealer, or the Internet Web sites of companies featured in the Resources section starting on page 122. Sign up for online newsletters to keep up-to-date on new products available for your embroidery creativity.

### Embroidery Machines

New embroidery machines are coming equipped with the latest of computer technology. From Windows-based processors to PC cards, keeping up can be a fun adventure!

Just like computers, technology never stands still. New embroidery machine models are introduced often. The purchase of embroidery machines and equipment from a local authorized dealer will ensure lessons, service, and help are provided. Test-drive machines with new technology and ask about trade-in policies. Familiarize yourself with new embroidery machine capabilities with and without

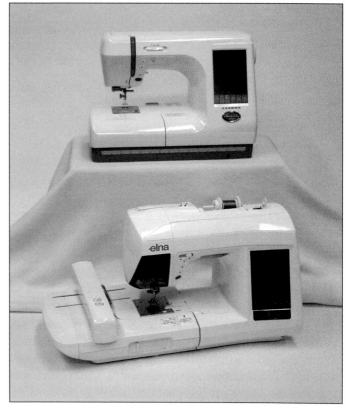

*Embroidery machines from Janome and Elna.*

software, how designs are transferred from the computer, and what software is compatible.

Most embroidery machines have on-board computers and some have update capabilities. Manufacturers usually provide updates downloadable from the Internet or through a local authorized dealer. Follow the manufacturer's instructions for updating an embroidery machine. Some machine models require an authorized dealer to complete the updates.

## Embroidery Designs

*An assortment of embroidery designs.*

Stock embroidery designs are created daily by a large variety of sources—both professional and amateur. Look for new designs at your local embroidery machine dealers, independent professional digitizing companies' Web sites, or on the Internet.

Designs are available on memory cards, disks, or downloadable from the Internet. Sold individually or in disk pack quantities, the availability varies amongst companies.

Always purchase designs in the format necessary for your embroidery machine. If your embroidery machine file format is not available, software can be purchased to aid the conversion from one file format to another. Or, conversion boxes are available for memory card conversions. For more information, refer to Design File Format Conversions starting on page 80.

## Embroidery Software

Embroidery software is evolving and new computer technology is paving the way. From automatic digitizing to resizing programs, software is available to make your embroidery more fun and creative.

Look for software updates at software manufacturer's Web sites or your local embroidery machine dealer. Depending on the dealer and the software, classes may be provided with the purchase. If not, look for tutorials that may be available with the purchase from independent educators.

It is illegal to share software—the same copyright laws govern software as well as embroidery designs. A security device is included with the purchase of most software packages. The security device must be attached to the computer for the software to function.

*An assortment of embroidery software.*

## Embroidery Stabilizers

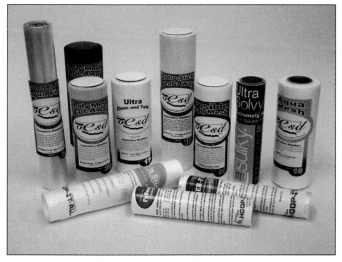

*An assortment of embroidery stabilizers.*

Stabilizers are a must-have item for embroidery. Stabilizers come in a variety of styles, content, colors, and package sizes. The most economical is to purchase stabilizers on rolls.

Be sure to follow the manufacturer's instructions for use.

### Water-Activated Adhesive

Available in a tear- or cut-away, the adhesive on the stabilizer is activated with water. To activate the adhesive, dampen a sponge, hoop the stabilizer, and lightly touch the hooped stabilizer with the sponge.

Once the adhesive is tacky, secure the item to be embroidered onto the stabilizer. For best results and holding power, allow the adhesive to dry before starting the embroidery process.

To remove the stabilizer, re-moisten it. While the stabilizer is still hooped, gently lift up on the embroidered item. Use a lightly damp sponge to re-moisten the stabilizer close to the edge of the fabric until the garment pulls away. It is important to not use too much water. Experiment with the stabilizer on a variety of fabrics to get use to the holding power.

### Fusible Mesh Cut-Away

Use a fusible mesh cut-away stabilizer on fabrics that stretch and can tolerate the heat of an iron. Adhere it to fabric with a low to medium iron temperature. Lightly iron the stabilizer to the back of fabric, hoop the fabric where the stabilizer is secured, and embroider the design. After the embroidery process, lift up on the excess stabilizer

and trim around the perimeter of the design. With a press cloth, iron on the backside of the design to fuse the stabilizer permanently to the fabric.

### Super Heavyweight Water-Soluble

Water-soluble stabilizers are available in a variety of weights—from light to super heavyweight. The thickest variety is perfect for free-standing lace-work. Embroider lace motifs directly onto one (or sometimes two) layer of super heavyweight water-soluble stabilizer. For difficult-to-hoop items, use a damp sponge to moisten hooped super heavy-weight water-soluble stabilizer. The stabilizer becomes sticky to adhere items during the embroidery process.

> When using a water-soluble stabilizer, always soak the embroidered project in water at least 4 hours. It is even better to soak 8-12 hours or overnight. You may not be able to see the stabilizer, but it may be inside the thread. Long soaks will remove it from inside your stitching.
>
> **— Robert Decker**

### Water-Soluble Mesh Cut-Away

This stabilizer can be used as a topping or a backing to keep washable fabrics stable during the embroidery process. Treat the stabilizer as a cut-away. After the embroidery process, launder or rinse thoroughly to remove the stabilizer. Use for towels embroidered with designs that have appropriate underlay stitches, lacework (use several thicknesses), and sheer woven fabrics where the designs match the weight of the fabric (not too dense).

### Appliqué Stabilizer

There are a multitude of products that can be used for securing appliqué fabrics to a project fabric. A single- or double-sided pressure-sensitive stabilizer can be used with the aid of a small craft iron. Press or iron the appliqué stabilizer to the back of the fabric. Trace the template onto the paper backing before releasing it from the fabric. Cut out the appliqué fabric, remove the paper backing, embroider the guideline for the appliqué onto the project, and secure the adhesive side of the appliqué fabric to the project within the embroidered guideline. Use a craft iron to permanently secure the appliqué fabric to the project fabric after the embroidery process.

*An assortment of powder and spray stabilizers.*

### Spray Stabilizer

When a tear-away or cut-away stabilizer will not work for embroidery, consider a spray stabilizer. It is perfect for washable lightweight and sheer fabrics. Spray the stabilizer onto the area to be embroidered and allow to almost dry. Use a dry iron to completely remove the moisture and "crisp" the fabric. Rinse fabric in lukewarm water to remove the stabilizer or launder after the embroidery process.

### Powder Adhesive

A powder adhesive with a non-stick pressing sheet can be used to secure appliqué fabrics. Using a template the shape of the appliqué, cut out the shape from fabric. On the appliqué fabric wrong side and over a paper plate, spritz fabric with water, and sprinkle powder adhesive onto the cut appliqué shape. Shake the excess powder from the appliqué. Embroider the guideline for the appliqué onto the project and remove the hoop from the machine. Secure the powder side of the appliqué fabric onto the project within the embroidered guideline. On an ironing surface, use a small craft iron to secure the appliqué fabric to the project fabric. Return the hoop to the machine and finish the embroidery process.

## Temporary Spray Adhesives

*An assortment of embroidery spray adhesives.*

Temporary spray adhesives help make the job of hooping fabric easier. Spray adhesives are extremely popular and can be used between layers of fabric and stabilizer to keep the layers from shifting while hooping, or with a hooped stabilizer to adhere fabric for embroidery.

The most common use is with a hooped stabilizer. Hoop the appropriate tear- or cut-away stabilizer for a project, spray the hooped stabilizer in a box, and secure the item to be embroidered to the stabilizer.

Always use adhesives in a well-ventilated area away from embroidery equipment. Spray lightly as to not gum up the needle.

## Embroidery Supplies

*An assortment of embroidery threads.*

### Threads

One can never have too many embroidery threads! Variegated threads provide a variety of colors on one spool or cone. From the hand-dyed look to theme colors, variegated thread is one way to add a lot of color to decorative designs with one spool of thread.

Thread manufacturers are continually updating thread colors, packaging sizes, thread types and more. Be sure to keep up with the latest in thread assortments at manufacturer's Web sites or at your local embroidery machine dealer.

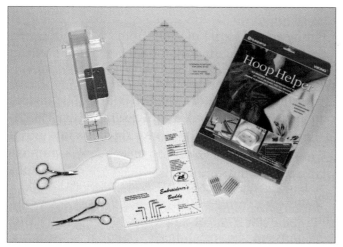

*An assortment of alignment guides, hooping aids, needles, and scissors.*

### Alignment Guides

Alignment guides help position embroidery designs onto fabric with ease. Guides can be used in conjunction with templates, allow for easy marking of center points, and can be used for repeat embroidery projects.

### Hooping Aids

The hooping of sheer fabrics can be difficult especially with larger hoops. Use specialty hooping helpers that hold the hoop secure, or provide a special tacky fabric to hold the fabric during the hooping and embroidery process.

### Needles

Non-stick and titanium needles are suggested for use with adhesive stabilizers and fabrics, such as vinyl, plastic, microfiber, and others that tend to stick to the needle. A non-stick needle has a coating to provide a smooth penetration of the needle through fabrics or stabilizers. A titanium needle is a very hard, does not heat up during high-speed stitching, and prevents the gumming up of the needle and thread. Both non-stick coated and titanium needles help to reduce the friction caused by high-speed embroidery.

### Scissors

There are a variety of scissors for embroidery, from duck-billed to curved tip to straight edge. Choose quality scissors that suit your embroidery needs. Curved tip embroidery scissors are helpful for trimming appliqué fabric or snipping threads close to the fabric. To keep scissors sharp, use paper scissors on stabilizers and sewing scissors on fabric.

### Miscellaneous

Here are a few more products to help make the embroidery process easier.

- Use a thread stand next to the embroidery machine with large cones or thread that requires distance to un-kink before entering the machine's tension guides.

- Use colorful permanent markers to touch up designs, where uneven tension causes bobbin threads to surface on a motif right side.

- Use watercolor paints to color fabric embroidered with redwork or quilting designs.

- Use a burning tool to trim away nylon organza or stabilizers from the edges of stand-alone dimensional designs.

- Use a mini-craft iron to secure appliqué fabrics to the project fabric during the embroidery process.

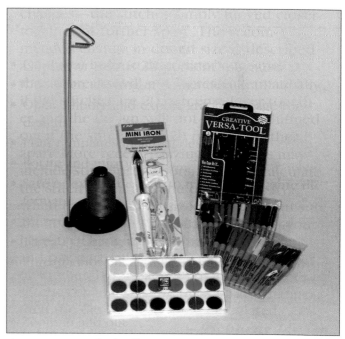

*An assortment of miscellaneous embroidery products.*

# *More* **Embroidery Hints and Tips**

One can never receive too much advice to ensure embroidery success. Here is a collection of embroidery hints and tips with additional suggestions from our industry experts.

## *Fabric Tips*

- Always pre-shrink fabrics or garments before embroidery to prevent designs from distorting.

- For dense designs on knits or sweaters, use organdy as the stabilizer and the topping. The stiffness of organdy will allow for a close trim next to the design in addition to staying with the fabric and design over time.

- To embroider on sheer or delicate fabrics, wrap the outer hoop with athletic tape to protect the fabric. Or, use a hooping aid that contains a special tacky material to help with fabric slippage. In embroidery software, lighten the stitch density and be careful not to use too much underlay (refer to Digitizing on page 54 for more information). The more needle penetrations means the stitches will pull on the fabric fibers. Use a lightweight thread, such as a 60- or 80-weight cotton or 50- to 60-weight rayon for best results. Embroider with the smallest needle possible, such as a 60/8 or 65/9.

## *Hoops and Hooping Tips*

- Use double-sided tape on the bottom of the inner hoop to hold the layers together during the hooping and embroidery process, especially when using large hoops. The tape will prevent fabric from slipping out of the hoop.

- Use small springs over the hoop tension screw to help hold the hoop open. The spring allows more flexibility and expands when using a variety of fabric thicknesses.

- It may be necessary to purchase additional hoops—especially standard sizes—for your embroidery machine. Hoops wear out over time. Keep stretched out hoops for use with heavier weight fabric. It is common to have more than one hoop size for use with spray adhesives and to keep clean for standard hooping.

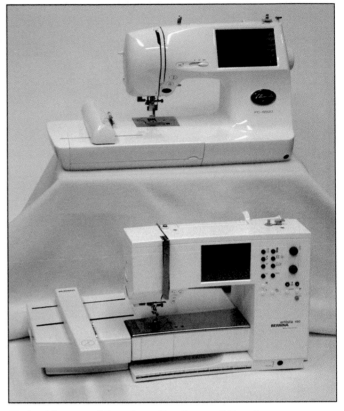

*Embroidery machines from Brother and Bernina.*

- Use the smallest hoop possible to accommodate a design. Too large of a hoop for small designs can cause registration difficulties and fabric pulling to the hoop center.

## *Using Embroidery Stabilizers*

- Use water-soluble stabilizer on top of a design with lots of jump stitches. The stabilizer keeps the stitches above the fabric and helps when clipping jump stitches, especially on fabric with a texture or nap.

- After embroidering stand-alone lace using a water-soluble stabilizer, hold it between two pieces of plastic canvas to keep the designs from distorting during the rinsing process. Use plastic twister ties to hold the canvas together.

- Tear-away stabilizers can pull on threads as it is removed from the embroidered design causing distortion. If the stabilizer is hard to remove, cut the stabilizer close to the design and allow frequent washings to remove the extraneous stabilizer.

Always select the proper stabilizer for the fabric and design. There is no "universal" product for all fabrics. Have multiple stabilizers on hand so that you always have what you need. To substitute for the proper stabilizer is to substitute poor quality for good quality stitch-outs.

*– Robert Decker*

## Using Embroidery Thread

- Use variegated thread for satin stitches around solid color appliqué fabric for a great visual detail. Variegated threads are also great for quilting outline designs or any design that has running or bean stitches. Watercolor variegated threads are wonderful for fill stitches, especially for textured leaves and items in nature that are textured.

- A 12-weight thread should be used with a large eye, large needle. Clean the machine frequently as this type of thread produces an abundant amount of lint during the embroidery process. Tighten the tension for thick thread to keep a more even machine stitch. Or, consider a heavier weight bobbin thread like a 60-weight cotton thread for standard machine embroidery or a 30-weight for lace. Experiment first before stitching on the final project.

- Use tweezers to pull up on jump stitches while trimming close to the design with curved embroidery scissors. The remaining thread "nub" will imbed into the design and offer a clean thread cut.

When having problems with unique threads, try a thread stand away from the machine—it can really help with some of the finicky tendency of specialty threads.

*– Nicky Bookout*

## Using Embroidery Needles

- After stitching a dense design, place a new needle in the machine to stitch the outline. This will ensure a clean design finish.

- Excessive thread loops and threads cut too short can be pushed to the backside of hooped fabric with a blunt edge large size (90/14 or greater) needle dulled from use.

- To embroider on satin, use a 70/10 ballpoint needle rather than a sharp needle, as a sharp will pierce the fabric fibers.

When using an adhesive stabilizer in the hoop, use a piece of lightweight tear-away stabilizer under the hoop to wipe the needle clean during the embroidery process. Or, consider using a titanium needle. This type of needle doesn't heat up as much and prevents a sticky needle.

*– Nicky Bookout*

- When changing needles, place a 3" x 5" index card over the needle hole of the machine to prevent the needle from slipping into the machine.

- Turn "off" thread cutting capabilities when using a wing needle. This can be accomplished on the touch-screen of the embroidery machine.

Needles, Needles, Needles! Always use a good needle! The life of a needle is much shorter when embroidering than sewing. Therefore, needles wear out faster. Buy needles in cost saving large volume 100 packs—the quality of your embroidery will be much better.

*– Robert Decker*

## General Embroidery Tips

- Schedule a machine tune-up at least once a year to keep it running optimally.

Be sure to test-stitch designs before embroidering on a project. The testing process is important to help you discover the best combination of stabilizer, thread, and fabric.

*– Annette Bailey*

- When creating templates for designs, create test-stitch samples with the same fabric as the project fabric. When a heavier weight fabric or a fabric that compresses is used for a project, the template should be made from the embroidered fabric rather than with a flat paper or fabric template. The loft and fabric compression will cause stitches to imbed into the fabric and misalignment. For best results, make a template from a copy of the embroidered fabric onto transparency film or trace the design onto the hoop template.

---

Test-stitch your embroidery samples on large pieces of fabric so you can incorporate the pieces into a future project
— *Nicky Bookout*

---

• For some embroidery applications, it may be necessary to pull the bobbin thread to the top of the fabric before starting the embroidery process. This technique is called a "rolling start" and is a way for the front and back of a design to look the same (towels, scarves, blankets, quilts). In addition, a rolling start will prevent the build up of stitches on the backside of the design. Fill bobbins in the thread colors for the design. Place the hooped fabric on the machine. While holding the needle thread, use the hand wheel to advance the first stitch until the needle thread brings up a loop of bobbin thread. Pull the bobbin thread up to the surface on top of the fabric (there will be two thread tails on top of the fabric). Stitch several stitches, stop the machine and trim both thread tails. At the end of the design or between color changes, repeat this process.

---

When embroidering on knit fabric, it is usually a good idea to place a piece on water-soluble stabilizer on top of the fabric. This will help the thread stay on top of the fabric and fine details will not be lost.
— *Robert Decker*

---

• To secure the stabilizer and fabric together, use an outline finishing stitch as the basting stitch. Embroider the outline first (usually the last segment of a design) in a thread color that matches the fabric, and then start the design over again. The outline will act as a holder for the rest of the design to stitch.

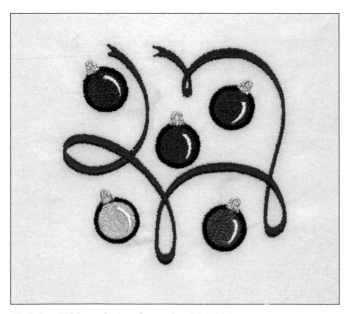

*Holiday Ribbon design from the CD-ROM.*

*Sports Balls design from the CD-ROM.*

# *More* Placement Pointers

Standard design placements are shown in *Embroidery Machine Essentials*. Go beyond standard placement and journey into a more fashionable approach to design placement.

Appliqué fabric in an allover pattern, alternating appliqué fabric colors and modifying the design orientation is a quick way to produce a project.

Adorn chair covers for all seasons on the front or back.

Decorate walls with pieced hangings over decorator rods.

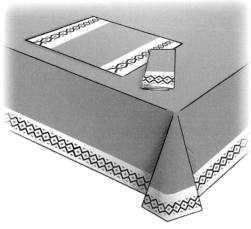

Coordinate table linens with borders by embroidering the fabric and then sewing the borders onto the table linens.

Personalization—from embroidery to monograms—makes a great gift.

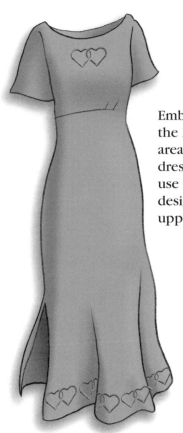

Embroider the lower area of a dress and use a single design at the upper edge.

Combine designs with machine stitches across the top of a shirt.

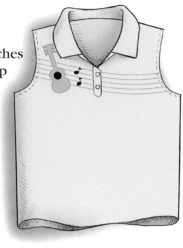

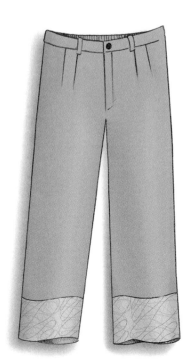

Vest points need accents, too. Edit a design for coordinating details.

Repeat a design with anticipated movement for visual impact.

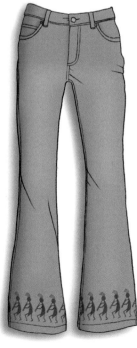

Top a cap off with customized designs and an iron-on appliqué over a heavy seam.

Open up the side or inside lower leg seam to embroider a repeat border. Then, close the area after embroidery.

Cut off the lower edge of cropped pants and add an allover embroidered fabric.

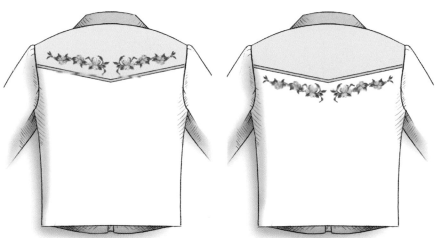

Embroider above or below a yoke.

A single design on the back shoulder area can be an elegant detail.

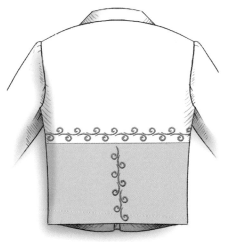

Embroider a pieced lower edge above and perpendicular to the seamline for a unique accent.

Embroider allover fabric, and then use the fabric for lower sleeve edges and cuffs, and for coordinating collars.

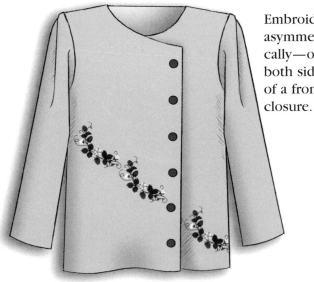

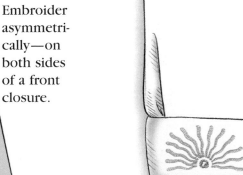

Embroider asymmetrically—on both sides of a front closure.

Center embroidery on sleeve cuffs or build a design into a lower sleeve edge treatment.

21

# Chapter 2

# Embroidery Machine Design Modifications

Some design changes can be made directly on an embroidery machine. Most can customize and resize designs, but there are limitations. Embroidery software increases design changing speed and capabilities. Determine if the best way to change a design is on the embroidery machine or through software designed specifically for your equipment.

If you need assistance determining the capabilities of your embroidery machine or software, consult the dealer that holds the warranty for your equipment. Some dealers hold monthly embroidery club meetings, provide personal consultations (sometimes for a fee), or have the latest tutorials from independent educators on utilizing embroidery machines.

> Look at embroidery as a problem-solving adventure. The more one knows about the physics of embroidery and how the embroidery machine works, the more options one has to reach a successful result.
> – *Mac Berg*

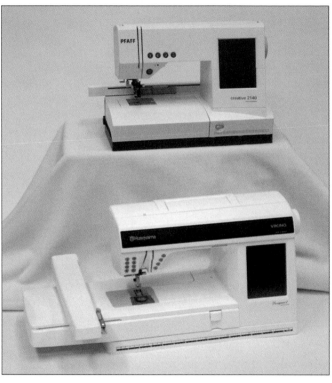

*Embroidery machines from Pfaff and Husqvarna Viking.*

## Touch Screen Features

The touch-screen is the central location for decision-making on an embroidery machine. The options available can vary from design orientation changes to combining multiple designs in a large hoop. Become familiar with the features available on the touch-screen by experimenting—push all the buttons to see what happens!

### The Active Workspace

Most embroidery machines have an area on the touch-screen where tasks can be performed. Some machines have screens that are 3" x 5" or larger with a multitude of selection buttons, while others have a small narrow viewing area where only minimal details are displayed.

*An active workspace on a Pfaff embroidery machine.*

From resizing to freehand digitizing, each machine manufacturer makes a different size touch-screen with variable features and capabilities. Depending on the machine, information may be available on multiple screens similar to software on a computer.

## Design Details

Once a design is loaded onto the embroidery machine, details such as the size, stitch count, design name, and thread colors can be viewed. Use this information when resizing designs, verifying thread colors, and determining the direction of the design.

## Grid and Hoop Display

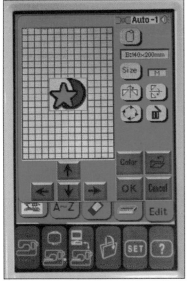
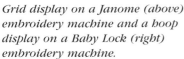
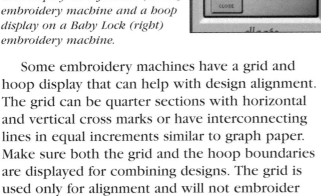

*Grid display on a Janome (above) embroidery machine and a hoop display on a Baby Lock (right) embroidery machine.*

Some embroidery machines have a grid and hoop display that can help with design alignment. The grid can be quarter sections with horizontal and vertical cross marks or have interconnecting lines in equal increments similar to graph paper. Make sure both the grid and the hoop boundaries are displayed for combining designs. The grid is used only for alignment and will not embroider onto projects.

## Arrows and Buttons

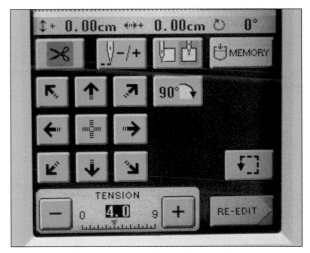

*Arrows and buttons on a Baby Lock embroidery machine.*

Use the directional arrows to navigate, select, and move designs within the hoop boundaries. The selection buttons are used to select tasks and to navigate through the screen pages.

## Highlighting Designs

Once a design has been loaded onto the embroidery machine, it must be highlighted in order to accept modification commands. Touch the design with a finger, stylus, directional arrows, or buttons. A box around the design usually indicates it is active and can be adjusted.

## Preferences

Customizing your embroidery machine personal preferences may be possible depending on the manufacturer. From the hoop sizes to the on-screen grid feature, some embroidery machines can be set with personal preferences. The preferences can be set so that each time the machine is turned "on" and "off" the

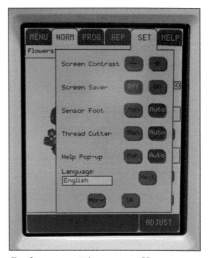

*Preference settings on a Husqvarna Viking embroidery machine.*

settings will remain consistent. This feature is helpful for keeping the grid feature visible. Refer to the machine owner's manual for help setting the personal preferences on your embroidery machine.

## Limited Design Creation

Some embroidery machines have the capabilities of on-screen, free-motion digitizing. With limited capabilities, it is possible to draw an image on the touch-screen with a stylus. Then, fill the image with thread colors and embroider the design. This feature is great for digitizing hand-drawn artwork and loosely embroidered random creations. Use your imagination as a guide.

## Open, Save, Transfer

Most embroidery machines can open or load embroidery designs from a memory card, disk, or directly from the computer through a cable. However, saving design modifications will depend on the embroidery machine capabilities. Once designs are combined or modified on-screen, some machines offer the option to save designs directly to the on-board computer, transferring modified designs to the computer, or saving to a disk or other media. For more information, refer to the instructions found in your embroidery machine user's manual.

# Customizing Designs

From mirroring to thread color changes, limited design customization can be performed on the embroidery machine.

## Design Orientation

*Rotating on an Elna embroidery machine.*

The most common design orientation changes are mirroring and rotating. Once a design has been loaded onto the embroidery machine, it can be rotated in degree increments and the mirroring can be from end-to-end or side-to-side. If the orientation changes are limited, it could mean that the design size is too large in one of the directions. Either switch to a larger hoop size or resize the design to fit.

## Combining Designs

Some machines with larger hoop sizes can combine multiple designs. To combine designs featured in this book, it will be necessary to use a hoop larger than a standard 4" square.

To combine designs, load the first design onto the embroidery machine. Move and rotate the design using the direction arrows or finger pressure to position the design on the grid. Open the next design and repeat the process. Some machines may load designs directly in the center of the hoop. Move them away from the center after loading to combine more designs. For more information on Combining Designs using software, refer to page 41.

*Combining designs on a Baby Lock embroidery machine.*

## Changing Thread Colors

Once a design has been loaded onto an embroidery machine, it may be possible to change thread colors. This is helpful when the designs and the suggested manufacturer thread colors do not coordinate. Use the manufacturer's guide to change the

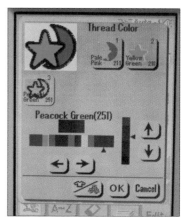

*Changing thread colors on a Janome embroidery machine.*

24

colors. Note that the thread colors do not have to be exact. Use your creative freedom to choose colors that look good and will embroider nicely on the project fabric.

## Lettering

In addition to combining designs, some machines can add letters or words to designs. Use built-in fonts to program one letter at a time in a straight line that can be arched or curved depending on the machine capabilities. The number of letters or words is limited to the hoop size and it may be necessary to embroider one word at a time. Some machines can set up multi-line words, while others are one line at a time. Rotate words to accommodate the largest amount of hoop space available. For more information on Lettering using software, refer to page 74.

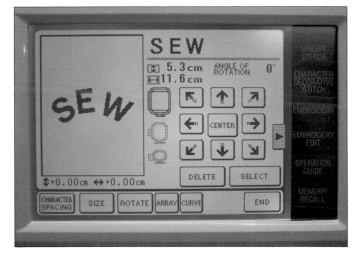

*Lettering on a Brother embroidery machine.*

---

## Resizing Designs

Most embroidery machines can reduce or enlarge a design 10 to 20 percent or more. However, most embroidery machines cannot increase or decrease the stitch count without a stitch processor that can recalculate stitches. These machines can lengthen and spread the stitches apart, which is great for a design that is too dense or a heavier thread is chosen to embroider a design. If a design needs to be reduced or enlarged more than 10 to 20 percent, additional software may be needed to add or reduce the stitch count while making size changes.

*A Brother embroidery machine touch-screen.*

To resize designs, load the design onto the embroidery machine. Increase or decrease the design size in degree increments with directional arrows or buttons until the design length and width is achieved.

### Stitch Count Changes

It is important to identify the location of the stitch count number on-screen, if available for your machine. The number may increase and decrease as the design is resized depending on the embroidery machine. If the stitch count does not change, then the stitches are only increasing or decreasing in length.

### Stitch Integrity

As designs are resized, it is important to keep the design stitches intact. Sometimes resizing causes the design to not stitch properly on fabric. It may be necessary to resize designs in software where more capabilities are possible, such as fixing errors or resizing without limitations. For more information on Resizing in software, refer to page 47.

# Chapter 3
# Introduction to Software

*An assortment of embroidery software packages.*

Why use embroidery software? While most embroidery machines have on-board computers that can provide some design customization, resizing, and even digitizing, the use of software will increase capabilities, creativity, and provide added design personalization to the embroidery experience.

Combining, editing, and creating decorative designs cannot be accomplished successfully without knowledge of the entire embroidery process. Successfully embroidering stock designs onto a variety of fabrics by simply altering embroidery notions is the first step in the embroidery process. The next step is to use software. An endless supply of creativity can be produced with the aid of an embroidery machine and accompanying software.

As one who quakes at the thought of learning a new computer skill, I've found that it's best to learn the basics of embroidery before tackling the variety of software programs on the market. As your knowledge of embroidery progresses, you begin to see a need for certain functions like separating design parts, combining designs, etc. and you can then learn the software that helps you achieve the results you want. As a new embroiderer, don't clutter your mind with the overwhelming software options before you know what you're doing or you'll never try anything!

— *Linda Griepentrog*

# Software Basics

What software is the easiest to use? One that is best suited for your embroidery needs and will work with your embroidery equipment.

This book is designed as a guide to help **with** the software process. It is not designed to show how to use brand-specific software. Therefore, it is vitally important to know your software and its capabilities.

## Using a Computer

Embroidery software needs a computer to operate. If you are new to the world of computers, take classes to help understand how a computer operates. Start with a basic introduction to computers. Take a class that will help you understand computer components, how to install software, the variety of ports that peripherals plug into, and more. Next, take a class about the Internet. Choose a class that will help you understand how to navigate, perform searches, download and more. Another class that would be helpful is a word processing class to help with the keyboard, shortcuts, and general typing skills. A computer graphics class will help in creating graphic images for digitizing.

It is vitally important to relax when using a computer. If you are tense, then it will be impossible for you to have fun with your computer creativity. If you do not understand something about your software, relax and take a deep breath before tackling problems. Spend a little time each day to learn more about the computer and the software.

> I f you are working at the computer or embroidery machine for extended periods of time, try to remember to stretch to alleviate a sore neck or shoulders. I set my digital timer to go off every 30 minutes. No matter what I'm in the middle of doing, I stop and do something else for a minute or so. Walk around the house, do some shoulder shrug stretches, take a bathroom break, or even just stand up and reach for the stars. These simple stretches are good for the body and the mind!
> — *Lisa Shaw*

If you have older computer equipment and software, it is still possible to perform basic embroidery software functions even though you might not

have all the timesaving features of a newer system. Before purchasing software, be sure the software and security devices will work with your computer operating system, ports, speed, and memory. Refer to the software specifications and the computer's owner's manual for more information on compatibility.

When considering the purchase of a new computer, purchase the best you can afford. Choose a machine with a large hard-drive, maximum memory, and a fast processor. A more powerful computer will allow for easier manipulation of designs, Internet access, downloading, saving, and software access.

> W hen getting new software, check to see if there is an Internet e-mail group or list you can join. These are great sources for ideas, tips on how to use a variety of software programs…and a great place to ask questions everyone has when they first start!
> — *Penny Muncaster-Jewell*

## How Software is Sold

*An assortment of bundled embroidery software packages.*

No two software packages are alike, but there are similarities. Some software packages are available in a bundle—a large software package with multiple embroidery functions, while other software components are available individually. Check with your dealer to identify software available for your embroidery machine. Most embroidery software can be used with a variety of machine formats—investigate software available from other embroidery machine manufacturers.

Bundled software programs have a variety of capabilities—customizing, editing, digitizing, and more—in one active window. Depending on the task, customizing designs and creating designs can be achieved without opening different software packages.

*An assortment of individual embroidery packages.*

Within individual software programs, the opening and closing of an active window is necessary to perform different embroidery software tasks. For example, combine designs using an individual customizing software program, and then digitize designs using another software program.

Getting to know software functionality, whether with bundled or individual software, is important. Knowing what part of software it takes to accomplish a specific task comes with understanding the basics of embroidery software.

## Trial Versions and Demo Disks

Sometimes it is possible to try a sample of embroidery software before purchasing a full version. Trial versions or demo disks may be available from a local embroidery software dealer or at the Web site of software manufacturers.

Downloadable trial versions may be available for a minimum number of days or minimum number of uses. Trial versions may not be full version and have limitations, but it is a great way to "try before you buy." Another way to test-drive software is to consult a local embroidery machine dealer for a hands-on demonstration.

## Security Devices

Commonly referred to as a "dongle," a security device is used to identify software ownership. Be careful with the security device, if it is lost or stolen, the device cannot be replaced. A new copy of the software must be purchased.

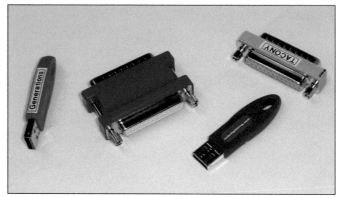

*An assortment of software security devices.*

In some cases, a cable connection between the computer and a read/writer box (for downloading designs to a card) or other embroidery peripheral may act as a security device as well. Most high-level embroidery software will not function without a security device. It will provide access to the software. In most cases, the security device is placed in a parallel or USB port depending on the connector. If multiple USB security devices are needed for an assortment of software, consider purchasing a USB hub.

## Installing Software

The installation of software onto a computer can be easy with the help of an installation guide found in a software user's guide, a quick set-up sheet, or on-screen assistance during the installation process. Read the installation instructions thoroughly before starting.

It may be necessary to attach a security device onto the computer before turning it on and installing software. If there is trouble during the set-up, read the troubleshooting section of the software user's guide, or consult the software or computer manufacturer for assistance.

## Peripherals and Ports

Peripherals are known as external devices. Printers, conversion boxes, scanners, external Zip® drive, and hard-drives are peripherals that can work with embroidery software. These devices help with

*An assortment of peripherals.*

template printing, the converting of designs from one format to another, scanning graphic images into the computer for the digitizing process, to store back-ups of designs, and so much more. Peripherals attach to the computer through a port on the front or back.

There are three ports where security devices, peripherals, or other devices can be attached to the computer—USB, parallel, or serial. These ports are located on the back or front of the computer and are available to plug items into. Software security devices plug directly into the ports. Peripherals or other devices are plugged into the port with a cable. It may be necessary to turn off the computer during the installation, or removal of peripherals or devices from the computer.

Most peripherals are available with a USB port connection. Purchase a USB hub to expand the number of ports available. A hub can support more than one USB security device and a variety of peripherals to prevent the plugging and unplugging of devices from a single USB port. It can transfer information to and from the computer faster than a parallel or serial port.

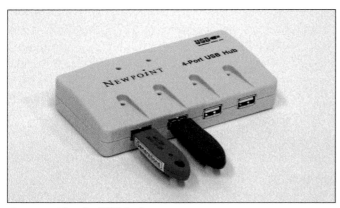

*An example of a USB hub.*

For back-up purposes, embroidery designs can be stored on a computer hard-drive, an external hard-drive, floppy disk, Zip disk, CD-ROM, or other media units. To provide a backup of data, choose a large capacity storage unit, such as a Zip disk or an external hard-drive.

## *Using a Mouse and Pointer*

The mouse and on-screen pointer are an integral part of using software. Just as shortcuts are used to speed up the software process, the mouse and pointer speed the use of on-screen icons and buttons. With a bit of eye-and-hand coordination, learn to use the mouse and pointer to utilize on-screen software components. Clicking on an object in an active window allows you to work with the data you see. A box around an object in embroidery software indicates that the object is active and awaits the next command.

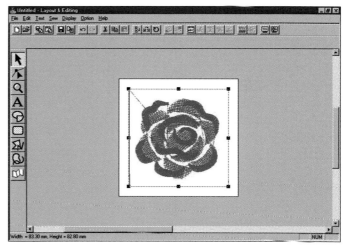

*Highlighted design in Brother software.*

There are usually two buttons on a mouse—a left and right button. Sometimes it is possible to right click on an on-screen object to prompt additional commands or tasks. To "Click and Drag" is the motion of keeping the left mouse button pressed on an object while moving the mouse to another location in the workspace. This is common practice when moving or shifting designs during the customization process. "Double-clicking" will provide additional options depending on the software. For more information about the mouse button capabilities within software, consult the software user's manual.

# Your Embroidery Software Choices

*An assortment of embroidery software packages.*

There are many categories of embroidery software available for customizing, editing, and creating decorative designs.

## Customizing

Used to combine, resize, mirror, rotate, reshape, and colorize embroidery designs, this software can combine lettering with decorative designs and customize elements to meet personal preferences. (For more information, refer to Customizing starting on page 40.)

## Stitch Editing

This type of software is designed to manipulate digitized stitches. From the editing of jump stitches to the splitting of large designs, the ability to break apart stitches to form new designs is the primary feature of a stitch editor. (For more information, refer to Stitch Editing starting on page 44.)

## Resizing

To enlarge or reduce designs while keeping the integrity of original designs is the main function of sizing software. Depending on the file format and the software compatibility, this type of program can alter the stitch count and density as it reduces or enlarges designs. (For more information, refer to Resizing starting on page 47.)

## Digitizing

This type of software will assist in the creation of decorative designs by assigning stitches to graphic images. The software is available with manual, semi-automatic, or fully automatic digitizing capabilities. (For more information, refer to Digitizing starting on page 54.)

## Cataloging

Organizing embroidery designs on the computer is this software's specialty. In addition, most cataloging software can convert designs to a multitude of formats, work with compressed files, and print design templates. (For more information, refer to Cataloging starting on page 70.)

## Lettering

Packed with a large selection of font styles and sizes, this software assists in the creation of words and letters. (For more information, refer to Lettering starting on page 74.)

## Cross Stitch

If you love the look of cross stitch but do not have time to stitch by hand, then this type of software is for you. Load a graphic image, assign stitches to the image, and then embroider. (For more information, refer to Cross Stitch starting on page 76.)

## Miscellaneous

From density changes to hooping help, there are a multitude of individual software packages available to help make embroidery easier. (For more information, refer to Other Software starting on page 79.)

Embroidery software has just the right tools to create exactly what I need to enhance or complement my sewing projects. The more proficient you become using embroidery software, the more power you have to express your unique creativity.

*– Bonnie Colonna*

## Embroidery Software Platforms

Embroidery software can either be "object-based" or "stitch-based" for customizing, editing, and creating decorative designs. Object-based software can select design sections by segments or elements (groups of stitches), where stitch-based software can only select design sections by individual stitches.

Once a graphic image is digitized and turned into stitches, the design becomes stitch-based and only minimal changes can be made. While the graphic design is being digitized it is in the object-based format and a multitude of changes can be made. To make large design changes to stitch-based designs, it is necessary to return to the object-based file format, or use software that can recognize and manipulate stitch-based files.

Some embroidery software can interpret stitch-based files and accurately turn stitch areas into objects that can be edited. Most digitizing software has multiple file formats—both object-based and stitch-based file formats.

## Linear Measurements

Most embroidery software measurements are preset in millimeters, but it is possible to change the preferences to inches. However, value increments are more accurate in millimeters than inches for embroidery measurements, including design density, stitch length, and width.

There are 25.4 mm in 1". To help with the millimeter transition, refer to the chart on the CD-ROM. Print the chart and keep it next to your computer when working with embroidery software.

Measurement rulers are great tools to have in embroidery software. This on-screen ruler is helpful in determining stitch lengths and design size. Located on several sides of the active window or as an optional tool, the ruler will help with the measurement in multiple design applications.

 ***A NOTE FROM JEANINE:***

To help with the visual conversion from inches and millimeters, purchase a ruler from an art supply store with inches on one edge and millimeters on the other.

# Learning Software

## Common Features

It is common to have overlapping features among an assortment of software. For example, lettering can be achieved in customizing software as well as individual specialty software. Get to know software by playing with all the buttons on-screen.

Many embroidery software packages have the following common features, tasks, and functions.

- Built-in help menu or tutorial to learn software
- Changeable default settings or properties
- File management: open, save, save as, close
- Keyboard shortcuts
- Object management: copy, cut, move, paste
- On-screen embroidery simulator
- On-screen grid and ruler for design placement accuracy

- On-screen hoop to determine boundaries
- On-screen viewing of design details
- Open, import, and export graphic images or designs
- Print templates in actual design size
- Rotate and mirror
- Save or export designs to multiple machine file formats
- Set preferences from millimeters to inches
- Thread charts from major manufacturers
- Thread color changing capabilities
- Undo and redo
- View design in real stitches (3-D)
- Zoom in and out

S et aside time to play with your software on a regular basis, rather than putting it off for several days of intensive sessions. This is the most effective way to learn software. Long sessions can put too much pressure on you, and often you get overloaded or stuck on one thing. A little bit at a time is the most effective way to learn software— you'll retain more and help to grow your skills with ease.

*— Penny Muncaster-Jewell*

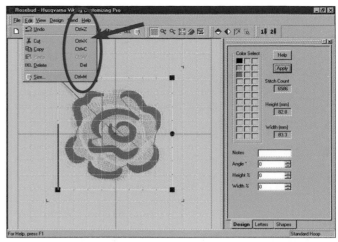

*Shortcuts in Husqvarna Viking software.*

## Keyboard Shortcuts

*A keyboard shortcut for "copy."*

This information is applicable for Windows-based computer keyboards only. The most common way to access software functions or computer commands is to select an icon in the Tool Bar, use the Menu Bar pull-down menu, or use a series of keystrokes. The fastest way is to use software functions or computer commands is with a series of keystrokes, commonly known as "shortcuts."

For example, to COPY an item into the computer "clipboard," hold down the CTRL button on the keyboard while selecting the letter "C." Each embroidery software package has product-specific "shortcut" keystrokes. Memorizing or using shortcuts frequently will speed the use of embroidery software.

Common shortcuts used for basic computer commands span most personal computer software. Some shortcut keys can be used to turn "on" or "off" a software function or computer command.

To identify software shortcuts, refer to the software manual or accompanying tutorials, or write down the common shortcuts found in the Menu Bar drop-down menus. Type and print a list of shortcuts in a word processing software program

that can be referred to frequently while using product-specific software. Each drop-down menu has a series of functions or commands, but not every function or command has a shortcut listed. Shortcut keystrokes are usually to the right of the function or command if one is available.

## On-Screen Features

Most software packages have a multitude of on-screen tasks that make the process of using software easier.

### Active Window

The active window is the area in which tasks can be performed. The active workspace consists of a blank area in an active window where design files can be imported, exported, saved, mirrored, and rotated. The size of an active workspace depends on the computer monitor size. The larger the monitor the more space that can be used for software tasks.

The perimeter of the active window features buttons, icons, and information used during the design alteration process. It is important to get to know all the parts of an active window.

The Title Bar is located at the top of the screen and usually contains the name of the software and the filename. The Menu Bar contains words below the Title Bar. The words can be selected to activate drop-down menus to perform assorted software specific tasks. The information can be accessed with a mouse or a series of keystrokes. The main Tool Bar is beneath the Menu bar and it contains a series of icons that can be used to perform common software tasks, or a series of frequently used commands. The Slider Bars enable the viewing of

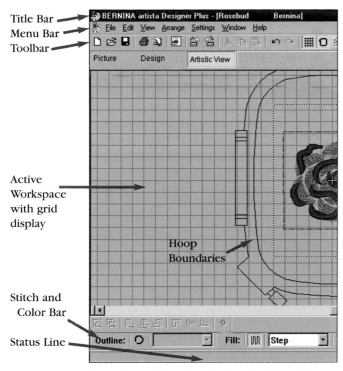

Title Bar
Menu Bar
Toolbar

Picture  Design  Artistic View

Active
Workspace
with grid
display

Hoop
Boundaries

Stitch and
Color Bar

Status Line

Outline: ○ ▼ Fill: ▥ Step ▼

*An active window in Bernina Artista software.*

the workspace in sections and usually found on the right side and bottom of the screen. Most software active windows contain additional information, such as design details, additional tool bars, and a host of function icons.

### A NOTE FROM JEANINE:

If an icon or function is "grayed out" on the computer screen, it means that the task is not available (yet). This feature was developed as a warning—that the task has already been completed, the task is not the next one available or the task is not available until you perform another task first. Determine why the icon or function is unavailable, or accomplish another task to activate the icon or function.

### Embroidery Simulator

The use of an on-screen embroidery simulator is to view a design as it stitches without the use of an embroidery machine. This feature is especially helpful to determine the design quality and to verify that components are in proper alignment before transferring it to an embroidery machine. The on-screen simulation of embroidery can be performed one stitch at a time, fast or slow, or hundreds of stitches

at a time depending on the software capabilities.

If a design has any quality or alignment issues, design editing may be necessary to ensure successful embroidery on fabric. The on-screen simulator should never take the place of embroidery on fabric as many variables can be discovered during the test-stitch process.

### Grid

The grid feature is similar to graph paper with interconnecting lines in equal increments. Use the on-screen grid feature to aid in alignment and placement accuracy when combining designs. This feature can be turned "on" or "off" and grid size can be adjusted within the software properties. For best results, keep the grid turned "on" and use this feature in conjunction with the hoop boundaries for design alignment.

### Hoop Boundaries

Knowing the perimeter of a specific size hoop in an active window can be important when combining or editing designs. Most software programs display a hoop outline or corner brackets to represent a specific hoop size. Select the appropriate hoop size before starting a project.

It may be possible to set a non-standard hoop size in the software preferences. To do so, measure the inner hoop area at the hoop notches and subtract 12.7mm (1/2") from each measurement to make sure the pressure foot has enough clearance to avoid hitting the hoop.

Cross marks and hoop notches are important to display within the hoop boundaries on-screen. These marks will help identify the hoop center that corresponds with the hoop notches for design alignment.

### Design Details

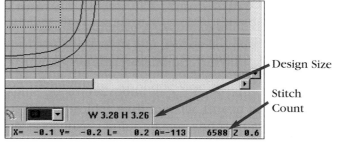

Design Size

Stitch
Count

W 3.28 H 3.26

X= -0.1 Y= -0.2 L= 0.2 A=-113 6588 Z 0.6

*Design details in Bernina Artista software.*

Most software can display information about a design on-screen within the active window. If the information is not on the screen, it can be found in one of the drop-down menus in the Menu Bar.

Knowing information about a design is important in the overall success of a project. For example, when resizing a design it is important to know if the stitch count changes while enlarging or reducing a design. Some design details to refer to on-screen may be thread colors, design size, or stitch or fill type. Use these details when customizing, editing, and creating decorative designs.

### Viewing Designs

The on-screen viewing of a design with real stitches, also known as "3-D," is helpful to determine if the end result of the embroidery will look good on fabric. If the design does not look complete on-screen, then changes can be made before the test-stitch process. For example, after generating stitches in digitizing software, view the design in real stitches to determine that the stitches formed will look good on fabric. This feature should never replace the test-stitch process as some underlying design problems may be detected during the test-stitch process.

> ### A NOTE FROM JEANINE:
> The realistic view with a fabric background is for visual purposes only. It is not for determining if designs will embroider properly and should never take the place of the test-stitch process.

### Background Changes

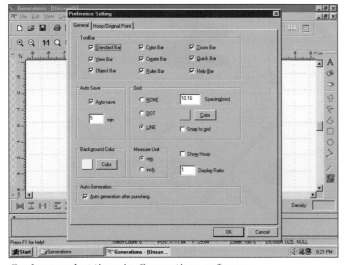

*Background options in Generations software.*

Most software packages offer the option of changing the active workspace background color

to view designs in 3-D. The most common color to use is white, but it could hinder the way a design will appear on the fabric. Choose a color similar to the fabric.

When viewing a design in 3-D, it could be possible to insert a background of the actual project fabric. Some software packages can allow fabric scanning to use as the background for realistic on-screen viewing.

Either way, this option should never replace the test-stitch process. This feature is available for choosing thread colors and to make sure the design will visually stitch well before the test-stitch process. Computer monitor colors could interfere with the end result of the thread color choices as well. Always test-stitch designs before stitching on the project fabric.

### File Management

All software can maintain files. From opening to saving, use software to perform a host of file management functions.

### Open, Import & Export

When getting to know embroidery software functions, select FILE [OPEN] to determine what file formats can be opened in the software, select FILE [IMPORT] to determine what file format can be imported into the software, and select FILE [EXPORT] to determine what file format the software can convert or transfer. The software manual will provide you with this information, but the action of going to these locations in the software may be quicker than looking in the manual.

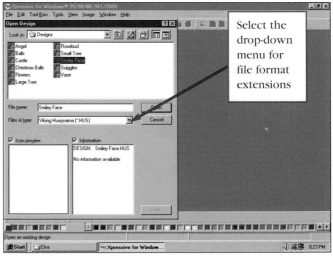

*Opening a design in Elna software.*

Most software will open designs in its "native" file format and import designs in "foreign" file formats. When it comes to opening or importing graphic images, the choices may be a bit different. Use FILE [OPEN], FILE [IMPORT], INSERT [PICTURE] or INSERT [IMAGE] from the Menu Bar depending on the software.

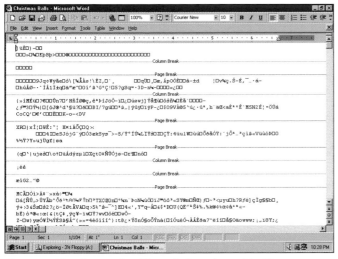

*An example of an embroidery design opened in the wrong software.*

---

### A NOTE FROM JEANINE:

**A**ppropriate software must be present to open an embroidery file. For example, a .HUS file format extension requires the Husqvarna Viking software to open the file. It is common to try to open files when downloading from the Internet. Save files to the hard-drive of the computer before opening designs in the appropriate embroidery software. If a series of gibberish text is in an active window when opening a file, this means the wrong software opened the file.

---

### *Saving Files*

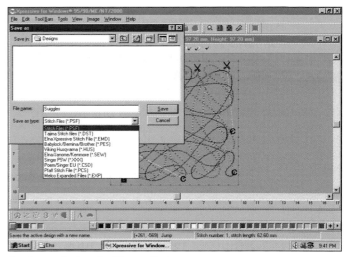

*Saving a design in Elna software.*

There are several ways to save a file. The FILE [SAVE] function from the Menu Bar, by selecting the icon that resembles a floppy disk, or a series of keyboard shortcuts will store the active window into a new or a current file. The first time a file is saved, the software will prompt for a location to save the file. Select a location on the computer that has been pre-determined. (For more information on organizing computer files, refer to Cataloging starting on page 70).

The FILE [SAVE AS] function from the Menu Bar will store the active window in a new file with a new name. This feature is used to copy an existing file rather than starting new, or when changes are made to an original file. It is extremely important to make a copy of the original file before making changes. Should there be the need to refer back to the original, the file will be intact.

Keep filenames simple. Save files often, or use an automatic saving feature if your embroidery software has this capability. For "universal" filename recognition in all embroidery machine and software, use an eight-letter name with a three-letter extension—FLOWER.HUS. This format will allow for easy identification of filenames across multiple platforms.

### Backing Up Files

It is a common practice to back-up designs onto disks or an external hard-drive. The investment of time to perform regular back-ups will prevent the accidental loss of information and valuable design files. Whatever system is created, be sure the task of backing up becomes routine and files are safely stored away from the computer. For more information about file storage refer to Cataloging starting on page 70.

## Common Tasks

There are several common tasks that can be performed using embroidery software. Use these tasks in conjunction with the other features of your software packages.

### Orientation Changes

A host of orientation changes can be made in software. The most common is the mirroring of designs from end-to-end, side-to-side, or a combination of both. Rotating designs can done manually or in degree increments.

### Rotate

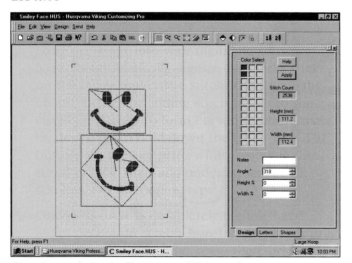

*Rotating a design in Husqvarna Viking software.*

The rotating of a design can be accomplished in most software by highlighting the design with the mouse pointer and using the "handles" surrounding the item to turn the design. Or, select "Rotate" from the Task Bar drop-down menu to choose the exact increment of rotational change.

The ability to rotate a design in degree increments can be useful when combining designs. Repositioning or reshaping a design may be necessary to "fit" an assortment of designs in the small confines of a hoop. The quality of the design remains intact during the rotation process.

### Mirror

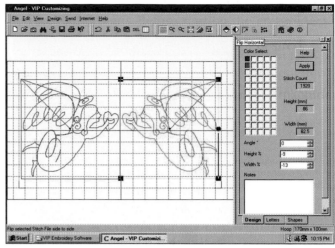

*Mirroring a design in Pfaff software.*

The mirroring of an object or design can be accomplished in most software. The software flips a design or image from either end-to-end or side-to-side.

The ability to mirror a design can be useful when combining designs or for design placement. Mirroring designs for the opposite sides of a project is a popular use for this feature.

### Thread Color Changes

The person who digitizes a design chooses the original thread colors. The colors are only recommendations and are the interpretation of the digitizer. The original colors can be changed in several ways using software. Choose thread colors by number from a drop-down menu of thread manufacturers and colors (Sulky; red), or by default color choices (yellow, purple, orange, etc.). For more information on thread color changes, refer to Customizing starting on page 40.

### Undo and Redo

The number of undo or redo changes can vary between software packages. Both of these features allow changes in software to be reversed or "undone." Be aware of how many undo options are available should a change to a file no longer be desired. Some software has limitations.

Save designs often, especially before making major changes to a file. Some software packages have drop-down menus of changes that can be "undone" at any stage—even between previous changes. A backward or forward curved arrow most commonly refers to this function in the Tool Bar options.

> Get past the "fear" of using embroidery software—you'll learn it quicker. Don't be afraid to push the buttons as "undo" is always an option!
>
> — *Nicky Bookout*

## Printing

Embroidery software can send a design image to the printer. A printed design can be used as a template or for design detail information. Depending on the software, a printed copy of a design can provide valuable information about the design, such as the size, thread colors, and hoop cross marks. Designs in "real size" can be used for templates printed onto transparency film for a see-through template, or onto paper for placement, design information or storage. Refer to *Embroidery Machine Essentials* for more information on making templates.

---

### A NOTE FROM JEANINE:

Purchase inexpensive "screen print" software to print the work-in-progress on a computer screen. The printing of a screen is helpful to remember software tasks. If a special feature in software is discovered, print a copy of the screen, write notes on the printed copy and file the information in a folder for future reference.

---

## Zoom In and Out

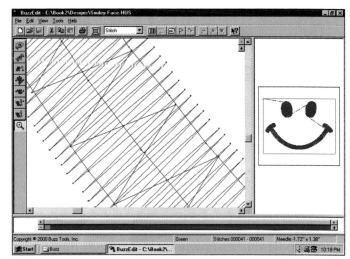

*The zoom feature in BuzzEdit.*

The only way to view designs or stitches close-up is to zoom in or out on objects or designs in an active window. The objects in an active window can be viewed larger or smaller than the original sizes—sometimes up to 800 percent. The zooming process does not enlarge a design or the stitches; it only allows for close-up views on the computer. This feature is helpful when combining designs to verify the designs are in proper alignment. In addition, the zoom feature will allow for extreme close up viewing of stitch points to add, move, adjust or delete one stitch at a time.

# Help and Information

*An assortment of helping aids.*

Look for help or information for embroidery software and equipment in these locations:

- Select the HELP Tool Bar in software
- Read accompanying user guide and instructional manuals
- Read and print files from software installation disks
- Go online to the software manufacturer's Web site
- View CD-ROM or book tutorials from independent educators
- Call the help-line of the software or machine manufacturer
- See your local dealer where software or equipment was purchased
- Contact friends and family with the same software or products
- Sign up and read Internet message boards
- Watch video(s) that accompany software or embroidery machines

Some software packages do not come with printed manuals. It is important to print the manuals from the software installation disks to obtain information on how to use the program. Keep the printed pages in a three-ring binder or notebook with sheet protectors.

> Find an embroidery buddy for every software program you use. This way you can work together to learn the software. This can be someone who lives locally or an Internet friend. It is more fun to work with others and when you get stuck, maybe your buddy can help!
>
> — *Penny Muncaster-Jewell*

## Technical Support Etiquette

When contacting Technical Support at embroidery software or machine manufacturers, have the following information ready as several questions will be asked.

1. What is the nature of the problem?
2. What is the embroidery machine make and model?
3. What is the computer processor speed?
4. How much memory is installed and how large is the hard-drive?
5. What software is being used? What is the version?
6. What is the computer operating system and version?

Technical support is only as good as the information provided. Be calm and provide as much information as possible. Ask questions if you do not understand what the technician is asking you or the answer to a problem.

## Updates and Upgrades

After installing software, check the version number. Even though the software was just purchased, it may be necessary to update the software at the manufacturer's Web site. Update and upgrades on software are performed regularly to keep up with the latest technology. Depending on when the retailer receives software or when the manufacturer's stock of older versions is depleted, updates may not have been added to the software you purchased. Check with the retailer to see if updates have been made to the software. It is common for the retailer to have update disks available or provide instructions for going to the manufacturer's Web site to download the current updates.

When major upgrades to operating systems (Windows or Macintosh) change the way your computer operates with embroidery software, it is because the system changes may be interfering with embroidery peripherals and software. It may be necessary to go to the Web site of the operating system manufacturer or your embroidery software manufacturer to download a patch (a problem fix) or an update.

Updates to software or embroidery machines usually come with a downloadable informational file. Print the file to learn the updated information. Save the printed information in a three-ring binder for future reference.

I f you are experiencing a problem with any software program, the first thing you should do is to check with the software manufacturer to make sure you have the latest version. To verify what version you are running on your computer, open the program and go to the HELP, then ABOUT menu option. This information screen will list the version you are currently using as well as other important information about the program.

*— Lisa Shaw*

# Design Transfer

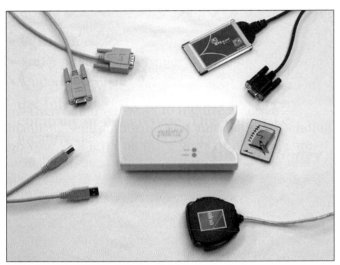

*An assortment of transfer media.*

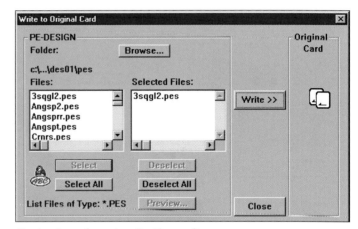

*Design transfer using Brother software.*

The transfer of designs from the computer to an embroidery machine can be achieved with software and transfer media, such as a cable, PC card, floppy disk, or read/writer box with a blank memory card. Use software that is compatible with your embroidery machine to transfer designs from the computer.

Open the design transfer portion of your embroidery machine compatible software. A blank page or field that requires filenames or designs will be needed to insert the designs to transfer. Select the designs from the computer hard-drive that require transferring. Once the designs or filenames are displayed on-screen, transfer the designs to the embroidery machine through one of the transfer medias. It is necessary to have the cable, PC card, CD-ROM, floppy disk, or read/writer box attached for this process. For more information about transferring designs for your specific equipment, refer to the software and embroidery machine owner's manual.

# Chapter 4

# Customizing, Stitch Editing, and Resizing

 he most common tasks in embroidery software are the customizing, stitch editing, and resizing of designs. While some design changes can be performed on the touch-screen of an embroidery machine, embroidery software will make the process faster, easier, and with more capabilities.

> ### A NOTE FROM JEANINE:
> The copyright laws govern modified designs, too. Even though changes made to a design or segments of a design are used in a combination, the personalized characteristics still fall under the copyright laws to protect the original creator of the design.

*A mixed-media wallhanging by Cindy Losekamp.*

## Customizing Designs

### What's Customizing?

Customizing is all about personalization—the combining and modifying of decorative designs. The customization of designs can be accomplished directly on fabric with templates and careful placement, on the touch-screen of an embroidery machine by combining and rotating designs, or in embroidery software with a click of a few buttons. By far, embroidery software makes the process of customization fun, fast and easy.

Customizing can be performed with software packages that may have some of these key features:

- Add design notes, lettering, and shapes
- Center designs
- Change thread colors
- Combine multiple designs or lettering
- Create a personal thread chart
- Group and ungroup designs
- Insert stock borders or frames
- Layout small to extra-large designs
- Print multiple hoop templates
- Resize designs with or without recalculation of stitches
- Save design with the proper hoop size
- Set custom hoop sizes
- Shape lettering—arch, bridge, circle, etc.
- Sort thread colors

## Combining Designs

Designs can be combined with customizing software. Combine stock designs with lettering or multiple designs to fit in larger hoops.

### Design Orientation Changes

Design mirroring and rotation are the easiest of orientation changes. These features help position designs in the assigned hoop field. Open or import a multiple of designs in place within the hoop boundaries. Rotate designs in degree increments, or mirror designs from top-to-bottom or side-to-side.

### Open or Import Multiple Designs

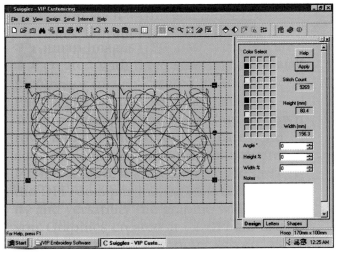

*Multiple designs in Pfaff software.*

Most customizing software can open or import multiple designs into an active workspace depending on the assigned hoop size. Open or import the first design by highlighting and moving the design to another location in the workspace. Then, open the next design.

Most software will open or import the design to the center of the hoop or workspace. Therefore, it is important to move the first design out of the way to accommodate the viewing of the next design. Continue opening or importing the designs to fit the hoop. After the designs have been opened or imported, highlight and arrange the orientation of designs to fit your personal specifications until the combined design is complete. Be sure to save often.

### Group, Ungroup, Center

When combining designs, most software packages require the "grouping" of designs before transferring to the embroidery machine. This task places a boundary "box" around all the elements in the active window and recognizes it as one file. If

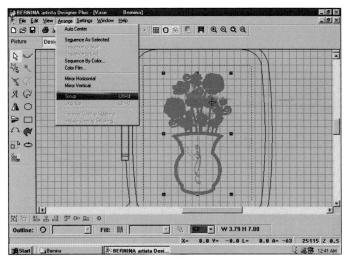

*The grouping of designs in Bernina software.*

changes need to be made to the "grouped" design, it may be necessary to "ungroup" the elements.

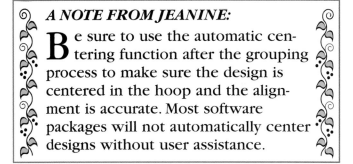

> ### A NOTE FROM JEANINE:
>
> Be sure to use the automatic centering function after the grouping process to make sure the design is centered in the hoop and the alignment is accurate. Most software packages will not automatically center designs without user assistance.

### Equipment Limitations

It is important to know the limitations of your embroidery equipment, such as the embroidery machine hoop field size, the computer embroidery software, the maximum design stitch count, and blank memory card. Some designs may have more stitches than a blank card can allow. It may be possible to combine too many designs and overload the system or machine requirements. Larger designs take longer to embroider and too many jumps can cause problems with tension and fabric distortion.

## Resizing designs

Resizing in customizing software can vary depending on the software by enlarging or reducing designs 10 to 20 percent or more. The stitch count may or may not change depending on the software. Look at the stitch count while resizing to determine if the stitch count is being altered.

Enlarging a design without stitch count changes will open up space between stitches. The use of a heavier weight thread could compensate for the space in the design when enlargement is close to 20 percent. Reducing a design without changing the stitch count will close up the space between stitches. The use of a lighter weight thread could compensate for the space in the design when reduced close to 20 percent. For more information on Resizing designs in software, refer to page 47.

## Lettering

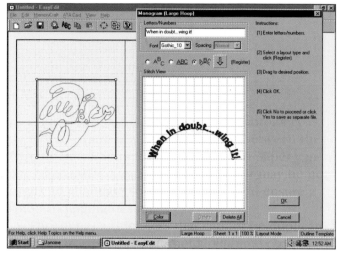

*Lettering in Janome software.*

Lettering is the combining of alphabetic characters and numbers with or without decorative designs. Stock fonts and computer True-type fonts can be used for Lettering. True-type fonts are those that are recognized by the computer or printer, while stock fonts are pre-digitized and ready for insertion into an active window.

Some software packages have fonts with minimal or no underlay stitches. Double check that underlay stitches are contained under the top thread, or load the design into editing or digitizing software to add the appropriate underlay. For more information about underlay stitches, refer to page 63.

Altering the space between the letters or using a variety of built-in baseline shapes can make the shaping of letters or words look good. Letters can be manipulated into a variety of shapes—arch, bridge, vertical, and more. In addition to lettering, shapes and frames can also be added to designs in an active window.

Refer to Appendix III for saying ideas that can be used with stock designs. For more information on using specialty lettering software, refer to page 116.

## Changing Thread Colors

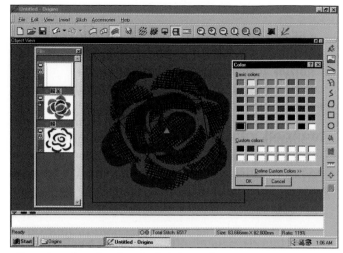

*Changing thread colors in Origins software.*

There are a variety of reasons why thread colors need to be changed, such as personal preference, to coordinate with the project fabric, or to match the manufacturer's suggestions. Original thread color choices are governed by digitizing professionals and the colors are recommendations to get you started.

Selecting thread colors is similar to using a coloring book. The thread colors are listed in software in order of appearance. Select a thread color and change it to another color from the software selection menu. Or, use a color strip feature to change the selected design segment, if applicable in software.

Colors can be chosen in several ways—by color number from thread manufacturer, by color category default (yellow, purple, orange, etc.), or by manually choosing threads from the design manufacturer's color guide.

### Thread Manufacturer Colors

There are a variety of color charts available from thread manufacturers. Often the thread color numbers are listed in customizing software. If a particular red is listed in the color guide and you do not have this exact shade, it is okay to substitute another color of red. The colors chosen by the manufacturer are only color guides. Substitute thread colors to match the fabric chosen for the project.

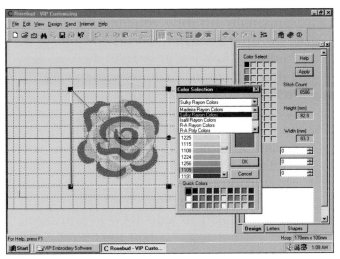

*Selecting manufacturer's thread colors in Pfaff software.*

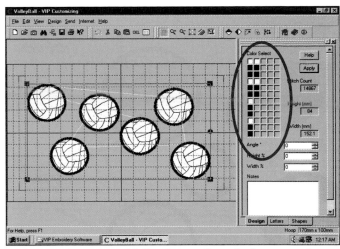

*Before a color sort in Pfaff software. Note the large number of black and white thread color changes.*

---

### A NOTE FROM JEANINE:

Be sure the latest version of software is loaded on your computer and embroidery machine. Sometimes there are updates to manufacturer color charts. The computer, as well as the embroidery machine, needs to be updated to accurately display thread color information.

---

Some software has the capabilities of creating a personal thread chart. Insert color numbers and manufacturer information into the software so when you "colorize" a design, you will be able to choose thread colors from your personal thread collection.

Colors may appear differently on the computer screen than on fabric. This may be the result of the computer properties. It may be necessary to set the computer color viewing properties to a higher number. For example, there are more colors in 32 bit (true colors) than there are in 16 bit (high colors)—choose 32 bit for the maximum number of screen colors.

### Color sort

A thread color sort combines "like" colors within a design to reduce the number of thread changes during stitching. After sorting the colors, the design will stitch in sequence with no two colors the same. This feature is especially helpful when combining two or more of the same designs into a larger hoop. Even though sorting colors is possible, many times the sort is not accurate and a design edit may be necessary.

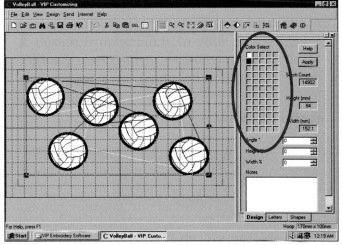

*After the color sort. There are only two thread color changes.*

If a color sort is not performed correctly, immediately "undo" the task. A duplicate thread color may need to be changed to another color prior to the sort to prevent combining colors that may not stitch in the proper sequence. Do not forget to change the color back to the original after the sort.

### Color Conversions

When converting a design to your embroidery machine file format, it may be necessary to run the design through a customizing software program to change the thread colors. If this is not done, the colors may not be accurately displayed on the embroidery machine.

At each embroidery machine stop, the next thread color listed on the embroidery machine may not be the appropriate color to use. Most design digitizers provide a numerical thread color listing to follow during the embroidery process. The listing may be provided with original disk packaging, need to be printed from a disk or downloaded file, or be printed on a design template from embroidery software. Use this listing as a guide to change thread colors or to use during the embroidery process.

### Changing the Stitch Order

After performing a color sort or combining designs, it may be necessary to change the order in which thread colors stitch. It may be necessary to change the stitch order in a stitch editing or digitizing software. Use the digitizer's thread color listing as a guide to move groups of stitches or entire thread colors into a more appropriate stitch sequence. This process will help to avoid excessive jump stitches and portions of designs that may be buried under other stitches.

### Design Segment Color Strip

Some software packages have an on-screen design segment color strip (similar to a 35mm film strip) feature. The color strip contains a group of boxes in a row that indicate the thread color stops and stitching order of a design. A multitude of design properties can be adjusted within the color strip depending on the software.

The most common use for a color strip is to change the stitch order and color of a design segment. The color strip will allow for the manual changing of the stitch order easily with the click of a mouse button. A host of other design property changes can be made with a color strip. See your user's manual for more details.

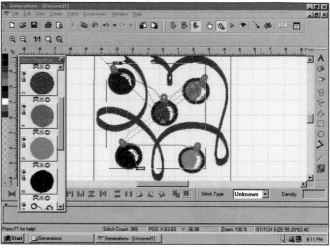

*A design segment color strip in Generations software.*

### A NOTE FROM JEANINE:

When combining designs, keep in mind the placement order and the stitch flow. As designs are opened or imported into software, the first design will embroider first, the second design will embroider next, etc. Open or import designs in stitch order for a smooth running design. Then, as a color sort is performed on the final combined design, the stitch flow should remain intact.

## Stitch Editing

### What's Stitch Editing?

Stitch editing can be as simple as moving misplaced stitches to as complex as eliminating design segments to form a new design. Stitch editing can be performed with software packages that may have some of these key features:

- Add design notes
- Change designs by colors, stitches, or objects
- Change stitch order
- Combine designs
- Insert, move, or delete stitches by stitch point (nodes)
- Edit one stitch at a time or in groups
- Insert, move and delete stitch commands

- Layout large designs
- Print multiple-hoop templates
- Re-route jump stitches
- Split designs for multiple hoopings
- Toggle between original design and adjusted design
- View color layers

To embroider on most fabrics takes embroidery knowledge, the appropriate supplies, and knowing when to edit designs to compensate for the variables. The test-stitch process will determine if design corrections are necessary or changes in supplies will be sufficient. For example, enlarging a design slightly and using more stabilizer may provide accurate compensation on sweatshirt fabric, but the alteration of underlay, density, and pull compensation on the computer may be the best choice for embroidery success.

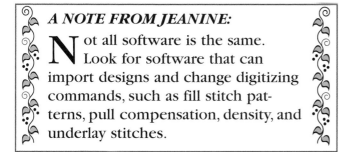

> ### A NOTE FROM JEANINE:
>
> N ot all software is the same. Look for software that can import designs and change digitizing commands, such as fill stitch patterns, pull compensation, density, and underlay stitches.

With the help of a basic stitch editing software, it is possible to add, delete, move, or modify embroidery stitches. These editing features can alter single stitches or groups of stitches. Use editing software to make design element changes, such as rerouting of jump stitches, deleting design segments.

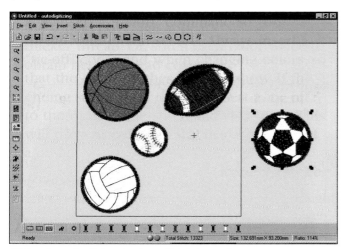

*Object-based editing in Autodigitizing software.*

In some software, editing stitches is easy. A thread color area in object-based software can be highlighted and only the stitches in the area will be edited. Conversely, a thread color area in stitch-based software can be highlight and all the stitches in the area (including stitches in the surrounding areas) will be edited. It is important to only highlight the stitches that are to be edited in both object-based and stitch-based software.

To make designs in stitch-based software easier to edit, use the "zoom" feature. While the design is enlarged on-screen, edit only the design segments necessary for the desired task.

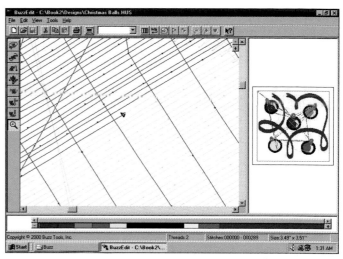

*Traveling through a design in BuzzEdit.*

Traveling through a design one stitch at a time is an easy way to eliminate stitches in stitch-based software. Locate the beginning of the design area to be deleted and use the delete or backspace button on the keyboard to eliminate one stitch at a time. Depending on how fast this feature works, the deletion of an area can move quickly.

## Stitch Point Changes

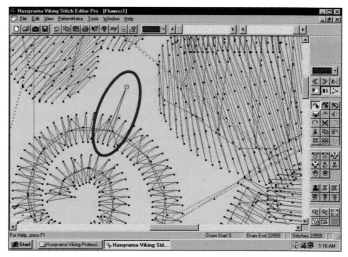

*Editing a stitch point in Husqvarna Viking software.*

To make stitch changes, use the stitch points (nodes) of a design to add, delete, move, or modify embroidery stitches. To move stitch points, select the node by clicking and holding the mouse pointer directly on the node; move it to a new location. If an entire section needs to be moved, circle the entire area with the mouse and pointer to highlight the area. Move the section to the desired location.

It is possible to add one stitch at a time in most editing software. If a large number of stitches need to be added, then the design must be transferred to a digitizing program to make changes. Some all-in-one-software programs have an advantage—multiple editing tasks can be performed in one open window eliminating the need to use other software programs.

## Stitch Command Changes

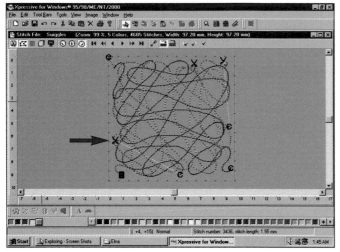

*The stitch commands in Elna software.*

Stops, starts, thread color changes, lock stitches, jump stitches, and a host of other stitch elements can be changed in editing software. Insert, delete, add, or move these elements using on-screen icons, menu options, or individually by stitch points in software. Choose logical locations for stitch command changes. For example, add color changes at the exact location by traveling through a design one stitch point at a time, to find the first stitch point for the new color. Insert the color change and lock stitches (to prevent the threads from unraveling).

## Editing and Combining Designs

Most embroidery software has multitasking capabilities. Some stitch editors can edit and customize designs. Edit designs by adding, deleting, or moving stitch segments, and then combine the designs using the same software.

Import or open a design, select a larger hoop size, and save the design with a new name. Highlight and delete the design segments that are not needed. Resave the design. Move the design from the hoop center and open the next design. Repeat the process. Next, use basic customizing features to copy, paste, rotate, mirror, and position the design element into the hoop field. Save the design when complete and transfer the design to the embroidery machine.

It is common to have overlapping embroidery features in software. Digitizing software is the most versatile.

## Registration Issues

Fabrics change the way a design embroiders. Should the design outlines be off during the test-stitch process, a variety of reasons may be the culprit—insufficient stabilizer, dull needle, or the wrong fabric. If you have all the correct embroidery notions and the design is still off, then a slight alteration to the pull compensation or reshaping the outline may be necessary to compensate for the fabric choices. Use editing or digitizing software to make these changes.

## Sew Simulator

Use a sew simulator to check for the proper use of design components, such as underlay and fill stitches. If a design does not have the proper components, then stitch editing may be necessary. Either bring a design into a stitch editor or import a design into digitizing software capable of altering the underlay, fill stitch, and properties.

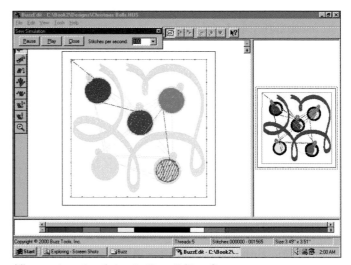

*The sewing simulator in BuzzEdit software.*

## Splitting Designs

Some software packages can split designs that are too large to fit in a standard size hoop. If stock design resizing is not an option, then it may be necessary to split a design to fit a specific hoop size. There are specialty hoops available to accommodate larger designs that can be embroidered in segments.

The split location can be manual or automatic depending on software and hoop capabilities. Always split designs in logical locations.

Embroidery machines and software can set up design splits in a multitude of ways. Some machines stop at the last stitch and stay to make it easier to align the parts. Some software provides an alignment line to ensure the sections come together.

Some software packages can set up multiple part designs for embroidery in larger hoops with position notches. The notches are used to slide the hoop lengthwise. In customizing software, set the hoop size, and then load or customize a design to fit the hoop boundaries. Save the design, transfer the design to the embroidery machine, and set up the hoop in the first notch. Most embroidery machines will indicate the placement of the notches for each design part. Embroider the design as directed by the on-board computer, moving or repositioning the hoop as required.

Check the software and embroidery machine user's manual for embroidering multiple part designs. For more information on design alignment, refer to *Embroidery Machine Essentials*.

## Resizing Designs

### *What's Resizing?*

Resizing enlarges or reduces stock designs. There are two ways to resize designs—with limits and without limits. Some embroidery machines and software have limitations and can only resize designs 10 to 20 percent without changing the stitch count. Other embroidery machines and software have no limitations, can size more than 20 percent, and will change the stitch count as the design size is enlarged or reduced.

Resizing can be accomplished with software packages that may have some of these key features:

- Adjust column density, fill density, and stitch length
- Set standard or custom hoop sizes
- Resize entire design or segments of design
- Resize to fit hoop limits
- Resize with or without recalculation of stitches

- Retain fill patterns
- Skew or reshape designs
- Stitch editing capabilities

When resizing, keep the design proportionate to the original design and within the hoop boundaries. To do so, highlight a design and use the surrounding "handles" to enlarge or reduce the design. Or, it is possible to enlarge or reduce a design by a percentage with an icon or a Task Bar menu option.

Some resizing programs do not change the density of designs when the size changes—the stitches simply moved closer together or further apart. The recommended change in design size is described as "plus or minus 20 percent" because thread breaks will not increase dramatically if the stitches are 20 percent closer together, and the design will not look too thinned out if the stitches are 20 percent further apart. More recent resizing programs may include stitch processors, which recalculate the stitch count and the design density when the design is resized. If you are unsure about which type of resizing software you have, try changing the size of the design, and pay particular attention to the number of stitches, before and after. If the number of stitches changes as the design size changes, then the density is being recalculated.

**— *Richards Jarden***

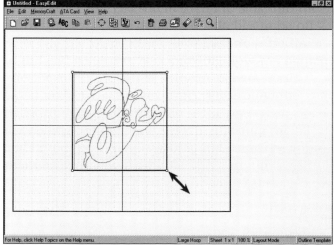

*Resizing in Janome software.*

## *Resizing With Limitations*

To size with limitations, the standard enlargement or reduction of a design—10 to 20 percent—can be useful to open and close the space between the stitches. This feature is helpful when using a variety of thread sizes and fabric thicknesses. Enlarge a design slightly for a thicker thread and reduce a design slightly for a thinner thread. Also, depending on the fabric used and how compact the stitches are, resizing can accommodate for the variation of fabric types used for embroidery.

## *Resizing Without Limitations*

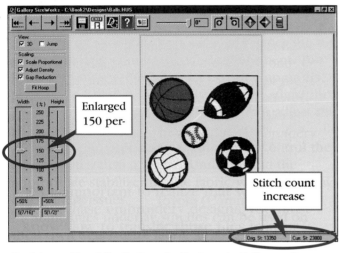

Enlarged 150 per-

Stitch count increase

*Resizing without limitations in Designer's Gallery software.*

Some software packages can enlarge or reduce designs without limitations by keeping design densities while changing the stitch count. The stitch count will increase or decrease as designs are resized. Depending on the resizing software, it may be necessary to open or import designs into a stitch editing or digitizing program to verify accuracy of changes made to the stitches. For best results, test-stitch designs before and after the resizing process to make sure the original design features are intact.

## *Editing Designs*

After the resizing process, it may be necessary to "tweak" a design. The resizing process is not always perfect. The adjustment of individual stitches, underlay, density, pull compensation, and stitch length may not provide accurate resizing results. It may be necessary to open or import designs into a stitch editing or digitizing software for changes.

Keep in mind that bigger is NOT always better. Sections of designs and/or fonts that contain satin stitches will not convert well when enlarged too much. You will either need to manually change distorted satin stitches to fill stitches or keep the design in the original size.

— *Regena Carlevaro*

## *Skewing Designs*

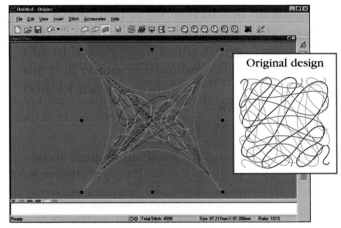

Original design

*Skewing of the Squiggles design in Origins software.*

Another feature of resizing is to "skew" a design—to purposely alter the design shape for decorative enhancement. Highlight an object and rotate or stretch the object out of shape to add some pizzazz to a design. Some software will change the stitches and the stitch count, while others will not.

## *Stitch Changes*

When resizing a design, jump stitches may be recognized as running stitches. Be aware of this and change the running stitches back to jump stitches after the resizing process.

When enlarging designs, some software packages automatically recognize long stitches and change satin stitches to fill stitches depending on the distance between stitch points. This feature provides for a smooth, efficient running design.

# An Exercise in Combining Designs

The designs available on the CD-ROM have customizing capabilities. From changing colors to combining designs, here's an exercise in customizing that will help you learn the basics. Use the Appliqué Vase and the Vase Flowers designs.

Width (mm) 96.3    Height (mm) 176.6    [Cancel]

Stitch Count 25068    Real Size % 61.9

*Combining designs in Viking software (3-D view).*

**NOTE:** To combine the designs included with this book, you must have a hoop for your embroidery machine larger than 4" square. The designs can be combined for use in a 5" x 7" or larger hoop. In addition, the software chosen to combine designs must have the appropriate size hoop measurements for your embroidery equipment.

1. Open your customizing software.

2. In the Menu Bar, start a new file.

3. Save the blank file with a new filename in the appropriate file format for your embroidery machine.

4. In the Menu Bar, select the appropriate hoop size for a 5" x 7" design project and turn the screen grid "on."

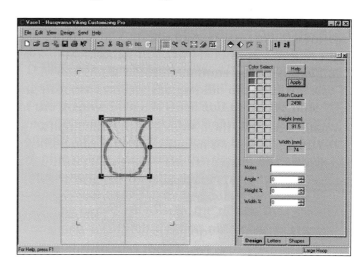

5. Open or import the Appliqué Vase design from the CD-ROM.

6. Highlight the design and move the design so the top edge of the vase is below the horizontal center axis.

7. Open or import the Vase Flowers design.

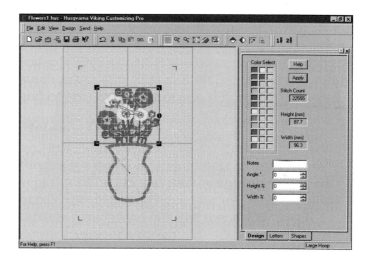

8. Highlight the design and move the design so the bottom edges of the flowers are just touching the top of the vase.

9. Highlight the Appliqué Vase again.

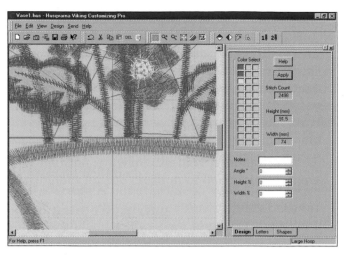

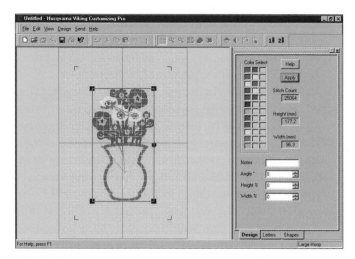

10. Use the "zoom" feature to view the positioning of the flower stems and vase top close-up.

11. Move the vase just over the lower edge of the flower stems.

12. Return the "zoom" feature to the screen normal size.

13. Save the design.

14. Use the "group" function in the Menu Bar options to combine the designs and create one file.

15. Make color changes to the design if desired.

16. Center the design in the hoop manually or with a Menu Bar option.

17. Save the design again.

18. Transfer the design to your embroidery machine and embroider the design.

Here are some more combinations using the designs on the CD-ROM.

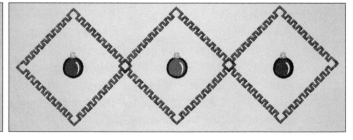

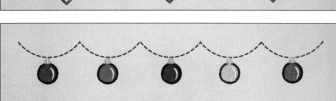
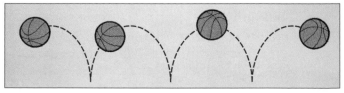

# An Exercise in Stitch Editing

The designs on the CD-ROM have stitch editing capabilities. Here's an exercise that will help you learn the basics. Use the Large Appliqué Tree and the Ornament Ribbon designs.

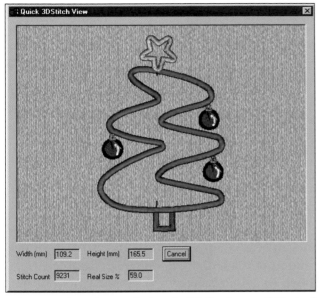

*Editing and combining designs in Pfaff software (3-D view).*

**NOTE:** Always make a copy of original design files before making any design changes.

1. Open your stitch editing software.

2. Open or import the Ornament Ribbon design from the CD-ROM.

3. Use the "Save As" feature to save a copy of the file to a new filename in the appropriate file format for your embroidery machine.

4. "Zoom" in on the design as much as possible to view it entirely in the active workspace.

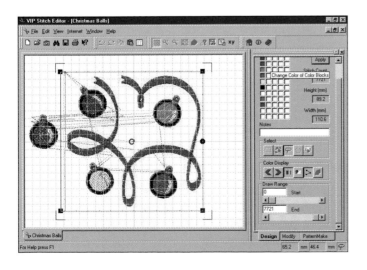

5. Depending on your software capabilities, eliminate all but the red center ornament. To do so, use the mouse and a lasso or freehand drawing tool to carefully draw around the red center ornament. Move it out of the way. Highlight and delete the remaining elements.

6. Or, forward through each color in the design and delete the design segments surrounding the red center ornament.

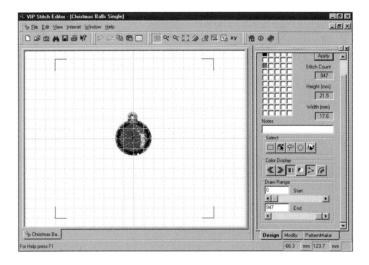

7. Center the red ornament.

8. Save the file.

9. Either continue in the same software or open your customizing software.

10. Start a new file.

11. Save the blank file with a new name in the appropriate file format for your embroidery machine.

12. In the Menu Bar, select the appropriate hoop size for a 5" x 7" design project and turn the screen grid "on."

13. Open or import the Large Appliqué Tree design from the CD-ROM.

14. Open and position three "new" single red ornament designs on the edges of the tree as shown.

15. Use the "zoom" feature to view the positioning of the ornament and tree close-up.

16. Return the "zoom" feature to the screen normal size.

17. Save the design.

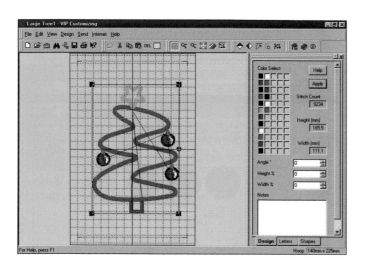

18. Use the "group" function in the Menu Bar options to combine the designs and create one file.

19. Make color changes to the design if desired.

20. Save the design again.

21. Transfer the design to your embroidery machine and embroider the design.

## Project Ideas

Use the designs on the included CD-ROM and your embroidery software to create some of these project ideas.

A pieced jacket with the Vase Flowers embroidered near the seamlines, is the perfect canvas for embroidery creativity. Embroider a matching shell to complement the jacket.

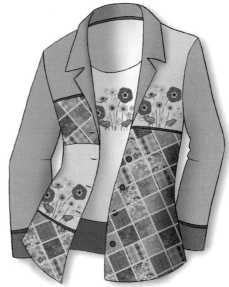

The angel design can be used to quilt a wall hanging. Use the rotate feature on your embroidery machine or software to make alignment easier without having to rotate the quilt.

Use customizing software to combine several Squiggles designs in a large hoop size. Embroider contrasting fabric for a jacket or shirt.

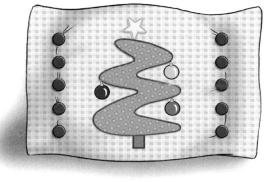

Use a stitch editor to separate the Sport Balls into five different files, separate the smile from the Smiley Face, and combine them all with your favorite lettering in customizing software.

Use a stitch editor to remove one of the ornaments from the Ornament Ribbon design into a separate file. Then, use customizing software to combine duplicate ornaments with the Large Appliqué Tree to make a holiday travel pillow. Instructions for creating the pillow can be found in *Embroidery Machine Essentials*.

Use a stitch editor to separate the Squiggles into four separate files. Embroider each one separately or combine the four individual designs in a large hooping system that layout 8" square designs for the center. Embroider the edge fabric in a continuous hooping system or on one long piece of fabric to piece with the center fabric to make the pillow.

Use the instructions for the Christmas Pillow to make a pieced Tree Skirt. Randomly embroider ornaments after the skirt is pieced to hold all the layers together.

Stitch up a fleece hat using segment 2 (texture stitches) of the Rose design. Use a stitch editor to separate the texture stitches from the satin stitches into a separate file. Embroider the texture stitches allover the fleece top and brim sections. More fleece texturing ideas can be found in *Embroidery Machine Essentials: Companion Project Series—Fleece Techniques.*

Instead of rotating the hoop, use the rotating feature on the embroidery machine touch-screen or in customizing software to sprinkle Smiley Faces on a shirt front. You can't help but to be happy during the creation of this fun project.

# Chapter 5
# Digitizing

Good digitizers understand embroidery. One who is serious about digitizing must understand the entire embroidery process, plus have experience embroidering on a variety of fabrics. This hands-on experience is important for the identifying and solving digitizing problems.

Digitizing is not an easy process; it takes years of experience to perfect the skill. Even with the easiest of automatic digitizing software packages, one cannot identify errors without having a background in the entire embroidery process.

What makes a good embroidery design? Outline running stitches that form just inside the outer edge of the design area, underlay stitches that form a solid foundation for which top stitches can lay, and top stitches of fill or satin stitches evenly laid to add beauty and dimension to the finished design. As the design embroiders, there should be a small number of jump stitches. These are signs of a well thought-out digitized design.

## What's Digitizing?

Digitizing is the art of turning graphic images into stitches that an embroidery machine can recognize. There are many digitizing software packages available—each with a different "style" of creating decorative designs. Digitizing principals and theories remain the same, but the software functions vary between manufacturers.

Digitizing can be performed with software packages that may have some of these key features:

- Automatic/manual pull compensation and density selections
- Blending and shading of stitches
- Color strip for viewing design segments
- Create new stitch patterns
- Digitize lettering from True Type fonts
- Edit one stitch at a time or in groups
- Fills: Novelty, complex, gradient, motif, etc.
- Gradient density

*Graphic Image*

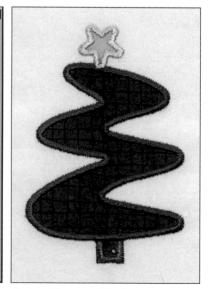

*Embroidery on Fabric*

Quick 3D Stitch View

Width (mm) 109.2    Height (mm) 165.5    Cancel

Stitch Count 9231    Real Size % 59.0

*Digitized Design*

- Group and ungroup
- Image cleanup, color reduction, sharpen
- Insert or fill holes within complex fill stitches
- Measuring tool
- Multiple digitizing methods: automatic, semi-automatic, manual, freehand
- Re-digitize existing designs
- Resequence colors, objects and stitch order
- Save object, outline, stitch information
- Scan artwork, image directly into software
- Select design properties based on fabric types
- Select fill patterns, thread colors
- Set entry and exit points
- Set fill angle in degrees
- Size designs with & without recalculation of stitches
- Split designs
- Stitch editing, customizing capabilities
- Stitch points: Add, change, delete, move
- Underlay, overlay

There are three ways to digitize a design—manually, semi-automatic, and automatic. Depending on your skill level, all three ways of digitizing are available in most digitizing software, but the end results vary. From flat looking embroidery to masterfully shaded and textured designs, time and experience make a difference in the final design.

## What's Needed?

A computer, digitizing software, graphic art software, scanner, printer, embroidery machine and supplies, color wheel, and projects ideas are needed to get started. Digitizing also requires a multitude of talents including:

- Knowledge of embroidery techniques
- Embroidery machine experience
- Computer knowledge and skills
- Sewing construction and fabric knowledge
- Detail oriented (likes to problem solve)
- Patience

Take time to understand the theory of digitizing. Start this process by taking classes and getting to know what the software can do for you.

Technically, embroidery machine stitching is hand embroidery that has been automated. Study books on hand embroidery and you will discover the origin of embroidery machine stitches. There are many common stitches—even the art of hand cross stitch has been automated to produce the look of handwork.

Embroidery machines, with the aid of digitizing software, are programmed to embroider designs with life-like stitches similar to hand work. Even the shading and blending of thread colors with hand stitches of various lengths can be duplicated with an embroidery machine.

> Relax. It is hard to digitize with a death grip on the mouse! Remember most software will allow changes and edits—you don't have to get it perfect the first time!
> — *Penny Muncaster-Jewell*

## The Digitizing Plan

*Example of a digitizing plan.*

A quality embroidery design is one that stops very little allowing a design to embroider smoothly. It is important to develop a digitizing plan—a design stitching sequence. Ask yourself these questions before starting. How should the design stitch to eliminate jump stitches and lower thread color changes? What design areas can stitch at the same time? Can running stitches connect areas and be buried under other stitches? What is the preferred order of stitching?

Plan! Plan! Plan! When digitizing, always plan the path of your design on paper before starting the digitizing process. This will save you from making mistakes, which might require you to start over.

**– Robert Decker**

When deciding on a digitizing plan, consider the fabric, design size, stabilizer, and thread requirements. Create a plan that takes into consideration the underlay, stitch density, and machine stitches to create a great looking design.

Layer thread colors on paper. List the colors from the background to the top. Be creative with jump stitch elimination and how much a thread color can embroider without stopping. Digitize the base thread color, and then add shadows and highlights on top.

### A NOTE FROM JEANINE:

There is no such thing as a complicated design, only a series of simple designs that make up one large design. Digitize a large design in sections to make the overall process easier. Or, break up designs into layered section and digitize each segment separately. Then, combine all layers by overlapping the sections to form one complete design.

## Stitch Commands

There are five basic embroidery commands—start, stitch, jump, stop, and end. The "start" command indicates the beginning of the design. The "stitch" command initiates the movement of the needle and the carriage (embroidery arm or pantograph) to form a stitch. The "stop" command directs the needle and carriage to stop for either an appliqué, thread color change, or a specialty technique. The "jump" command indicates the time to move the carriage and hoop to another location and continue stitching. The "end" command indicates the design is finished.

Digitizing software must be able to communicate these commands to the embroidery machine. To successfully embroider a design, commands must have parameters, such as the density, pull com-

pensation, underlay stitches, and a variety of basic finishing stitches to embroider correctly.

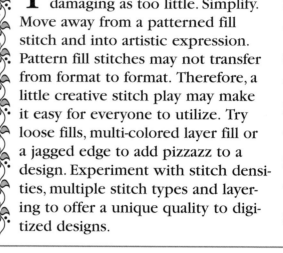

### A NOTE FROM JEANINE:

Too much creative stitchery is as damaging as too little. Simplify. Move away from a patterned fill stitch and into artistic expression. Pattern fill stitches may not transfer from format to format. Therefore, a little creative stitch play may make it easy for everyone to utilize. Try loose fills, multi-colored layer fill or a jagged edge to add pizzazz to a design. Experiment with stitch densities, multiple stitch types and layering to offer a unique quality to digitized designs.

## Graphic Images

Starting with quality graphic images can make the digitizing process easier. Graphic image requirements change between software packages. Some software accepts images in outline format only, where others accept solid color images similar to a cartoon.

### File Types

Determine the type of graphic image your digitizing software packages can open or import—outlines, solid color or solid black and white images. Most digitizing software packages can import or open BMP, WMF, or JPG graphic image file formats.

There are two types of image file types—bitmap and vector.

### Bitmap Image

A bitmap image is made of pixels (dots) that make blocks of color. The pixels are measured by the number of dots per inch. A bitmap image is viewed as one whole object. When enlarging a bitmap image, the larger the image the more jagged the edges. This makes for difficult digitizing. Bring a bitmap image into digitizing software the exact size. Some software may allow the size to be increased or decreased without losing some of the definition. Or, digitize the design in the original size and increase the design after the digitizing process.

*Sample of an enlarged bitmap image.*

*Sample of an enlarged vector image..*

Bitmap Images (JPG, BMP, TIF, etc.) are created with fixed sizes and are usually pictures or images created in Adobe Photoshop or Paint software packages. When a bitmap image is sized up or down, rows and columns of dots (squares) are added or deleted. This can make the resulting image have a jagged edge. The greater the DPI (dots per inch), the greater the quality and versatility the graphic will have for you. Graphics created at 72 DPI are usually just for use on the computer screen. As the DPI goes up, so does the amount of memory it takes up. A large image at 300 DPI can require a very large amount of hard disk space to store and memory (RAM) to display and print.

*– Melinda Bylow*

Vector Images (AI, WMF, EPS, etc.) are made with applications, such as Adobe Illustrator, Corel Draw or Macromedia Freehand, and are mathematically made with joined lines and shapes. The pieces can be arranged, grouped, and sized in relation to each other without losing clarity. Lines, curves, and patterns will look their best no matter how you manipulate or size the images. The memory required for a vector graphic file is significantly less than a bitmap file. Vector graphics are a bit harder to create and only a few applications can edit them.

*– Melinda Bylow*

## Vector Image

A vector image is made of outlines and shapes with smooth edges and computers can recognize a vector image easily. Each object in a vector image can be selected and edited independently rather than a bitmap image that is one whole object. The resizing of a vector image in graphic art software will make digitizing easier as the lines remain smooth.

Enlarge or reduce vector images in graphic art software before starting the digitizing process.

## Artwork

Original hand-drawn artwork is the best source for digitized designs. Other image sources can be used for digitizing, but copyright laws may prohibit the use. Check with the owner of images or artwork for use restrictions. Look for artwork to digitize in software packages, coloring books, needlework transfer sheets, or graphic images prepared specifically for embroidery.

Learn to work with vector images if your digitizing software accepts them. Geometric shapes are easiest to create. Start off by experimenting with basic shapes to understand working with vector images.

*A variety of artwork sources.*

Hand drawn art is on paper and embroidery is on fabric—there is a large difference between the two mediums. Sometimes the detail on paper cannot be translated into thread stitches. It may be necessary to eliminate some of the detail to ensure a smooth-running design.

Thread has a thickness that cannot be duplicated from an artist's drawing. The details are going to look different. Thread does not blend like paint, which makes the duplication of shading more difficult.

Try to duplicate an artist's drawing, painting, or photograph with color markers or pencils in the same thickness as thread. This will provide an understanding of how to digitize a design close to lifelike. Spend time working with graphic images before the digitizing process. Plan the design by tracing or printing an image and determine the types of stitches to use for the design.

---

### A NOTE FROM JEANINE:

Duplicate a picture or image on a copy machine with a lighter setting. Then, use color markers or pencils to draw in the stitches as if digitizing the design. This will give you practice on determining the stitch path and thread colors for the design.

---

Once a graphic image is in digitizing software, it may be necessary to put the image though a software specific "image processor." This function prepares the image for digitizing and provides the software with information about it. The process may resize the original image, omit the background color, determine the maximum colors, and select the image type.

Some software packages can view images in a split screen beside the design while digitizing. It is helpful to have the original image nearby during the digitizing process either printed or on-screen for reference. Many times the "zoom" feature is used and the entire image is not in view.

Most digitizing software can insert a graphic image on-screen for use as a digitizing guide or template. The image will be in the background of the active workspace during the digitizing process. A template can help form accurate embroidery stitches and can be removed after the digitizing process. Poor quality graphic images should be inserted into digitizing software as a guide or template and manually digitized.

### Scanning Artwork

Scanners can be used to transfer hand-drawn art to the computer for the digitizing process. It can be scanned directly into digitizing software, or saved on the computer hard-drive.

Once the image is on the computer, the file should be opened in graphic art software. Touch up the image if needed. Connect all the lines with on-screen tools, and adjust the line thickness. For best results, scan artwork into the computer the original size.

### Cleaning Up Artwork

Minor changes to artwork may be needed before the digitizing process. Brightness, contrast, or intensity features in software can be used to adjust the balance between light and dark areas of an image. The "sharpen" feature can be used to accentuate the edges of an image or to brighten details. Noise reduction can be used to remove unwanted specks, image details, or spots on the background of an image. Bitmap images can form jagged edges during the resizing process, therefore it may be necessary to clean up the edges.

Simplify graphic images as much as possible and reduce the number of colors. If there is too much detail, the design will take a long time to digitize and embroider. Instead, add a bit of flair to a design with the use of thread shading and texture.

Some digitizing software packages have the ability to make simple changes to original artwork. Otherwise it is necessary to use an external program to edit the graphic image to prepare it for digitizing.

If you are unhappy with the digitizing results, the problem may be with the original artwork. Start with a "clean" graphic image—outlines that are an even width and clear colors without smudges or uneven tones. Some graphic artwork programs are designed specifically for embroiders. Choose one that prepares or edits graphic images with easy-to-use drawing tools. Look for added features, such as the exporting of images directly to digitizing software, importing of WMF files, or placement of True Type Font text.

**– Lisa Shaw**

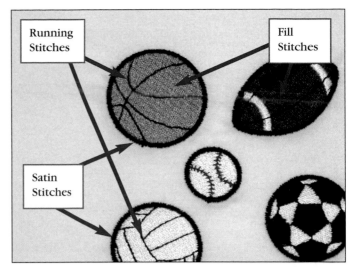

*Stitch-type example.*

## Stitch Options

There are three types of stitches for embroidery—running, satin, and fill. All digitizing software packages can recognize and manipulate these three stitches to produce embroidery designs. On most embroidery machines, the longer the stitch length, the longer the design run-time and the shorter the stitch length, the shorter the run-time.

When creating or editing a design, I like to keep a protractor by my computer so I know at a glance what angle a fill stitch is, or what angle I want to rotate my design.

**– Nancy Zieman**

### Running Stitches

Running stitches can be used alone or together with other stitches. Used alone, the stitches can be used for quilting designs, free motion decorative designs, and metal designs. Used together, the stitches form underlay, outline, and can travel between same color areas in a design.

The stitches can be single, double, or triple by traveling back and forth along a line. Known as a "bean" stitch, a triple stitch is used for outlining designs or providing details to already laid design stitches.

A running stitch that outlines an image just inside the perimeter of a design can provide a clean, crisp edge to fill stitch areas. Underlay running stitches formed at another angle to the final fill stitches will create the ideal foundation. Sometimes it may be necessary to run multiple layers of underlay in opposing directions to the final fill stitches to offset heavily textured fabric.

It's so easy to create a redwork or quilt design from scratch. In your digitizing software, use your line tool to draw a design, select the triple stitch and you're done!

**– Nicky Bookout**

Consider eliminating outline stitches for lifelike features—not every design is in need of an outline running or satin stitches. For example, a lion's mane is not flat. In reality, the hairs have a jagged protruding unevenness. An outline would make the edge look flat where added shading or some manually set stitches would be more lifelike.

### Satin Stitches

Satin stitches are the most luxurious of embroidery stitches. A meticulously laid column of satin stitches with a high-sheen rayon thread can dress up any detail. The larger the satin stitches the more radiant the color, but slower the design will embroider.

Satin stitches should not be narrower than 1mm or larger than 6-9mm, depending on the capabilities of the embroidery machine and the weight of the fabric. Limit the stitch width for slower embroidery machines. Lighter-weight fabrics should use a narrower width than heavier-weight fabric. It is never advisable to use a heavier weight stabilizer on lighter fabric to compensate for stitch incompatibility. It is better to adjust the stitches to compensate for the fabric.

Underlay stitching is extremely important to use under satin stitches. Select a single center run underlay for a narrow satin stitch, a zigzag underlay for a medium satin stitch, and a full edge run and step zigzag underlay for larger satin stitches. For more information on underlay stitches, refer to page 63.

### Fill Stitches

One of the many ways to cover an area in embroidery is to use "fill" stitches. These stitches utilize running stitches sewn parallel and close together to fill in a design area. There are a multitude of patterns than can be incorporated into the fill to create a texture. The fill can be contoured, complex, motif, and radial.

Basic embroidery designs transfer the best between embroidery formats. Add complex fill pattern and specialty stitches, and foreign file formats will not understand the machine codes or language. When this happens, the software or embroidery machine will convert the fancy patterns and stitches to plain stitches resulting in loss of stitches and design definition.

> Choose your fill patterns carefully. They can either add or detract from your design. They are there to add beauty to your design, not to be the focal point of the design and draw the eye to them.
>
> – Robert Decker

If several layers of fill stitches are used, leave holes of lighter fill for the second layer to cover up. If multiple layers are to be stitched for a raised effect, lighten the density on all the layers for overall good coverage. Bulletproof embroidery is not advisable!

One way to eliminate the stitch count in a design is to make an area of fill an appliqué. Turn a stock design into an appliqué by removing the fill stitch, adding a running stitch outline, add a stop/color change at the beginning and end of the outline, add zigzag underlay stitches, and then add the satin finishing stitches. If fill stitches are surrounded by satin stitches, only add the outline placement guide stitches and set the satin stitch width to 3mm. Be sure underlay stitches are present under the satin stitches.

To highlight a fill section with thread, add a layer of low-density fill or manually digitize a light layer of stitches. These stitches could run parallel to the decorative top stitch to allow the threads to blend with each other or at slightly different angles to

prevent the stitches from disappearing into the previously laid stitches.

Use a color wheel when layering or blending a fill area with several thickness of low-density fill. Most color wheels have information about combining colors. For example, mixing red and blue will create purple. By substituting the colors on the

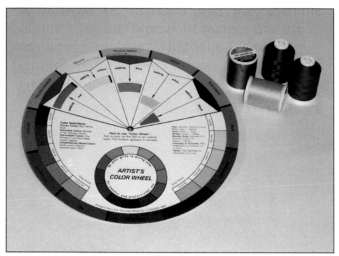

*A color wheel is helpful for blending thread colors*

wheel with thread, you will have the perfect shading tool. If a graphic image is not a cartoon, but an object from nature, then the blending process will be instrumental in bringing realistic features to fabric.

### Jump Stitches

Jump stitches are necessary for traveling between two design parts when needle and thread penetrations into fabric are not needed. These stitches can be short, long, or imbedded depending on the distance between objects. Lock stitches are necessary before and after a jump stitch to hold the thread in place.

Imbedded jump stitches are those that are too short to trim. In lettering, imbedded stitches are used to "hop" from one letter to another in a small or compact spaced word or name.

Jump stitches may turn into stitches when resizing designs. To reinstate a jump stitch, zoom in and remove the stitch points, nodes, or dots that have been added to the jump stitch line. Jump stitches in software are usually dashed lines. Remove the points until the dashes are reinstated.

Trim jump stitches often during the embroidery process.

> The weakness of every design is jump stitches. Every design must start with a jump stitch, but try not to use any jump stitches after the first one. If you must insert a jump stitch, make it as long as possible so that it is easy to trim.
>
> **— Robert Decker**

## Lock Stitches

A lock stitch holds thread in place on the fabric with compact stitches that overlap each other. Commonly referred to as a tie-on, tie-in, tack-down, or tie-off, the stitches are used to form a knot between the top and bottom thread to keep the threads from unraveling. Lock stitches are used between color changes, and before/after jump stitches.

> At the end of a satin area, be sure to insert a "tie-off" command so your thread will remain secure. Always insert a "tie-off" command when changing colors, so that the extra stitches will not show. If the ending stitch is on the left, insert a "tie-off" to the right of the stitch and visa versa. This will prevent compact stitches at the end of a design.
>
> **— Robert Decker**

## Edge Finishes

The finishing stitches of a design can be a satin, outline, or motif. Outline or bean stitches are the most common for highlighting design details. A thin satin-stitch border can help to cover design distortion flaws and offer room for fill alignment errors. Jagged-edge satin stitches and motif stitches are "fun" finishes for appliqué.

Use outlines to define segments of a design. Simple shading may not be enough to define the difference between image shapes. A single running stitch in a complimentary color can be used to define design areas.

Sometimes narrow satin column stitches can be embroidered at an angle to produce a longer stitch. If a satin stitch runs over previous laid stitches, then digitize stitches in an opposing direction to prevent jagged or hidden threads.

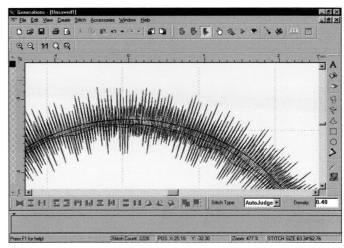

*A "fun" finish for appliqué in Generations software.*

> ### A NOTE FROM JEANINE:
>
> Experiment with an assortment of decorative edge finishes. Use a jagged-edge design finish if available for your software. Design edges do not always need to be straight or even!

## Motif Stitches

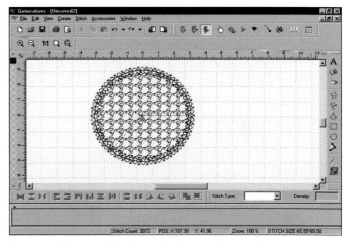

*Sample of the motif stitches in Generations software*

Some software can produce motif stitches. These are stitches that resemble fancy sewing machine stitches. The possibilities are endless for combining motif outline stitches with standard fill stitches or for using motif stitches as fill stitches. A cross stitch pattern is a commonly used motif fill. Experiment using motif stitches in place of outline and fill stitches.

### Cleaning Up Stitches

The removal of stitches shorter than a predetermined stitch length can be helpful to clean up a design, help it run smoother, and reduce the stitch count. Short compact stitches tend to cause embroidery problems especially thread and needle breaks, and unpleasant embroidery results. This feature may be pre-set in software preferences and a finishing step that should not be ignored. Be sure that lock stitches are not removed in the process.

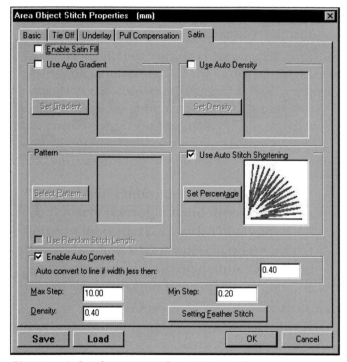

*Shorten stitches function in Generations software.*

Use a "shorten stitches" software function to alter the stitches around a curves or corners. This feature changes compact stitches to more open and varied stitch lengths in sharp curves or corners.

Some software is programmed to recognize column fill and satin stitch variables. The software will change too long of satin stitches to fill stitches greater than a pre-determined width. Conversely, stitches that are too small and compact will be removed.

> Take time to learn the keyboard short cuts in your digitizing software instruction manual. This will help you save time when you are manually digitizing designs.
> — *Regena Carlevaro*

### Fabric Properties

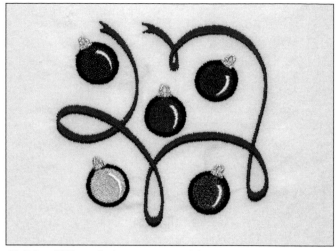

*Holiday Ribbon design on woven fabric.*

The multitude of fabric properties, from stretch to woven, affect the way a design is digitized. A design digitized for woven fabric will embroider differently on knit fabric. Learn how to alter designs to compensate for fabric changes.

While the changing of stabilizers will help the end result, small changes in the design properties will create better embroidery. Finding a happy medium is a digitizer's challenge.

The use of underlay in combination with the proper stabilizer will prove to be a successful marriage between design and fabric. If a design embroiders poorly, it is important to understand the characteristics of fabric and what stabilizers are best to use for the changes in fabric. Changes can be made to the design to compensate for the fabric unpredictability.

Get to know the texture and feel of fabric. First, feel the fabric—is it smooth, textured, thick, or thin. Determine what stabilizer is best for the fabric. Next, consider the design characteristics and how much underlay will be needed to support the design on the fabric.

Fabric stretch indicates the need for cut-away stabilizer and the appropriate underlay to create a foundation for the design. Fabric texture indicates the need for cut-away stabilizer, a topping, maybe multiple underlay layers, and more density to prevent the fabric from "popping up" through the stitches. Fabric that is light in weight requires a lightweight thread, needle, stabilizer, and stitches.

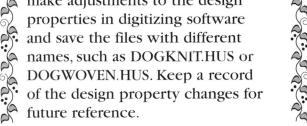

### A NOTE FROM JEANINE:

When digitizing stock designs for use on a variety of fabrics, choose stitches suitable for knit fabrics. This way the design will have the appropriate outline, underlay, fill and satin stitch densities for a knit and woven fabrics.

Keep a notebook of digitizing properties for fabrics you like to embroider. Once you have found a successful combination of design, fabric, thread, stabilizer, underlay, density, and push/pull compensation, then put this information in the notebook for future reference. Some software packages can save parameters for certain fabrics. Others have pre-set parameters to make the digitizing process easier as it eliminates guess work and provides for more digitizing fun.

### A NOTE FROM JEANINE:

When embroidering the same design on different fabrics, make adjustments to the design properties in digitizing software and save the files with different names, such as DOGKNIT.HUS or DOGWOVEN.HUS. Keep a record of the design property changes for future reference.

### Fleece

Digitizing for fleece or similar high-loft fabrics takes extra care. The stitches tend to sink into the fabric and can cause outlines or stitches to be off. Selecting the right design for the fabric is pertinent to the end result, but also knowing how to compensate for the fabric loft in software is beneficial. Good underlay is the key especially around the outside edges. Distorting the shape on screen depending on the fabric stretch, adjusting the fill and border pull compensation, and using the appropriate weight of cut-away stabilizer are the keys to successfully digitizing on this luscious fabric.

### Test-Stitching

Stay away from poor quality fabric for embroidery and test-stitching designs. A perfectly digitized design will fail a test-stitch on poor quality fabric.

Always test-stitch a design on fabric the same or similar to the project.

Just because a design looks good on screen doesn't mean it is going to stitch out properly. It may be necessary to adjust the design in software, or adjust the stabilizer and hooping method. A design may need to be distorted on-screen for the design to embroider properly on fabric. Always refer back to your basic embroidery skills to determine how to solve design problems.

## Underlay Stitches

Underlay stitches are the foundation of an embroidery design. These stitches are used to hold the fabric and stabilizer layers together, to keep the fabric pile from "popping up" through the stitches, to help hold the design registration intact, and to keep the design edges smoothly stitched.

The fabric type, stabilizer, and design combination determine the underlay. It contains short running stitches placed under top finishing stitches to help prevent the fabric from shifting during the embroidery process. Design depth can be achieved with more underlay to add personality to designs. The buildup of stitches under the fill and satin stitches will keep embroidery raised off the base fabric instead of lying flat.

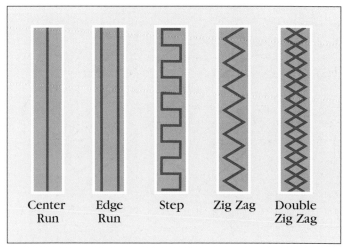

| Center Run | Edge Run | Step | Zig Zag | Double Zig Zag |

*Underlay for satin stitches.*

Underlay stitches can be placed manually or automatically depending on the capabilities of your digitizing software. The most common underlay stitch types are center run, edge run, step, zigzag, double zigzag, or a combination. Software defaults may not suit the fabric and design needs. Adjust the stitch type when necessary. It may also be necessary to manually add underlay stitches into design areas lacking support.

> Remember your underlayment! When digitizing, you will need approximately 20-30 percent as much thread below the surface as you do on top. This is even more important when digitizing designs to be sewn on knit fabrics.
>
> *– Robert Decker*

Underlay is important under fill stitches to prevent fabric puckering and usually run in a different direction than the top stitches. For even more stabilization, use two layers of light underlay in a crosshatch formation and run the top stitches in the opposite direction. Underlay stitches have a purpose and should be uniformly laid under the top stitches to help control the fabric movement. To keep embroidery stitches from drawing up or distorting the fabric, it may be necessary to adjust the pull compensation, add more underlay, or adjust the stitch length.

A knit will require more underlay to control the fabric stretch than a woven. Underlay and the appropriate stabilizer for the fabric will solve many embroidery issues.

Sometimes underlay stitches can be used on their own to texturize fabric. Insert or add a stop and tack down stitches at the beginning and end of the underlay otherwise threads can pull out.

Underlay stitches increase the stitch count and embroidery time to designs, but is well worth the added stitches for a successful embroidered design.

## Pull Compensation

When embroidering a design, the needle, thread, and the hoop movement cause a push and pull effect on the fabric. These movements cause fabric distortion unless the proper underlay and stabilizer are used to protect the fabric and stitches. It is important to understand the effects these properties have on fabric to completely understand the digitizing process.

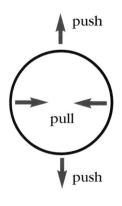

Adding pull compensation to stitches makes an area wider, which will reduce the distortion of fab-

ric. Embroidery stitches that move horizontally may need to have the pull compensation widened. It is also necessary to shorten the object shape because the stitches will push the fabric vertically.

Depending on the fabric stretch, satin, and fill stitches distort in the opposite direction top stitches are laid. Most fabric stretches either across the grain or on the bias. Pull compensation affects the way fabric stretches.

> Remember when digitizing a design, satin stitches can scrunch up the fabric due to the pull of the thread and fill stitches stretch out the fabric due to the additional thread being added to the fabric. Therefore, the pull compensation must be adjusted for both of these actions.
>
> *– Robert Decker*

Study designs and learn to recognize pull compensation problems before the test-stitch process. In software, when pull compensation is used, there are times when fill stitches form outside the borders. Deliberate distortion of designs to compensate for fabric push and pull is a necessity. Sometimes compensation can be with the appropriate fabric stabilizer and tweaking of the design in software.

## Density

The design density refers to the space between stitches and determines how close stitches are to each other during the embroidery process. A smooth fabric requires less density than a textured fabric. The

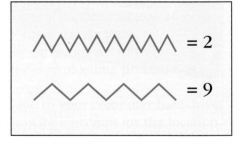

higher the number, the lower the density and more space between the stitches. The lower the number, the higher the density and less space between the stitches. Increase the fill density by decreasing the value.

Thin satin stitch columns require fewer stitches for good coverage than a wider satin stitch column. A smooth stable fabric requires less density than a knit or fleece. Overdoing the density may result in thread and needle breaks or puckering.

If fabric fibers poke through stitches, the density is too low. Increasing the density will increase the number of stitches and decrease the space between the stitches compacting fibers into fabric. Density can also be adjusted for the underlay stitches in some software packages.

Forget the rule about staying within the lines. Good embroidery designs often have overlapped sections, which compensate for stitch density and type of fabric being used.

— *Regena Carlevaro*

## Threads

Sometimes it is necessary to make modifications to designs for thread variables. With the variety of threads available, some threads can provide digitizing challenges and delights.

*An assortment of embroidery thread.*

### Color Limitations

Use nine thread colors or less for digitizing to accommodate most embroidery machine software and equipment. Check your software manual for the maximum number of color changes per design.

To determine color limitations before the digitizing process, evaluate the graphic image. If the size of the graphic image is small and there are nine colors, eliminate some of the color details using software. If the size of the design is large and there are nine colors, the size of the design most likely can accommodate all the colors.

If a design must have more color changes, then it may be necessary to split the design into two files. Open and stitch the first nine colors. Then, open and stitch the second file as if continuing with the next thread. If you made any hoop movements or adjustments for the first file, make the same adjustments for the second file.

### Thread Sheen

Threads with a high sheen can be used to an advantage by digitizing with angles to reflect the light. Digitizing with one thread color can yield successful results when changing the stitch angle. For example, instead of two different color greens for a leaf, edit the design for one color with two different stitch angles. The light will hit the thread differently and create the illusion of two different colors.

### Metallic Threads

The adjustment of designs for use with metallic threads is a necessity. Use a lower density to prevent thread breaks and use the appropriate sized needle specifically designed for use with metallic threads. Avoid using metallic threads in heavily detailed areas of a design.

Metallic threads require 5 to 10 percent fewer stitches than standard 40-weight thread. Avoid small, compact and lock stitches to prevent thread breaks. Increase the design size slightly without changing the stitch count to allow metallic threads some breathing room.

To embroider with metallic thread in fill stitch areas, digitize a color change and stop after the underlay stitches before the fill stitches begin. During embroidery, sew the underlay stitches with a thread color that matches the project fabric, and then change to a metallic thread to embroider the fill stitches. This provides metallic threads with a smooth surface to embroider.

Use a thread stand away from the embroidery machine to allow the metallic threads to unwind smoothly and prevent thread breakage. If necessary, use an additional horizontal thread holder to pull the threads off a spool or cone in the direction the thread was wound.

## Software Specifics

Digitizing software can have a multitude of capabilities for the creation of decorative designs.

### Automatic Digitizing

*An assortment of automatic digitizing software packages.*

Automatic design digitizing software can differ among manufacturers. Depending on the software specifics, automatic digitizing software can recognize graphic images and assign stitches to an object with minimal commands. Some software packages have additional features that can further modify or enhance assigned stitches.

> When working with an auto-digitizing software, the most important step is to start with a solid color, clean image, free of specks or smudges.
>
> **— Nancy Zieman**

Automatic digitizing software produces embroidery designs using a series of default stitch values. Depending on the software capabilities, the default settings or "preferences" can be modified. After assigning stitches to a graphic image and the initial test stitch process, determine if additional design changes are required and the preferences that can be modified. Refer to the user's manual for more information.

Minimal automatic digitizing commands may render a design flat in appearance as a computer is determining basic information about the design. Some preference editing may be necessary to input

variables the computer cannot possibly know, such as the fabric type, stabilizer, thread, and their relationship to the design.

It is important to know how fabric and thread interacts with a design. Automatic digitizing software can identify graphic blocks to fill with stitches, but it requires a knowledgeable user to make sure the blocks are filled with appropriate underlay, pull compensation, and density to produce a quality design.

Some automatic digitizing software can also be used for other capabilities, such as customizing, stitch editing, lettering, and thread color changes. Determine the design file formats that can be opened or imported into the software for these and other design modifications.

### Manually Digitizing

The manual digitizing of designs is an art form. Skilled digitizers know exactly where, how many, and in what order to place stitch points for a perfectly digitized design. One has a lot of control over the end result of a design by learning the manually digitizing process.

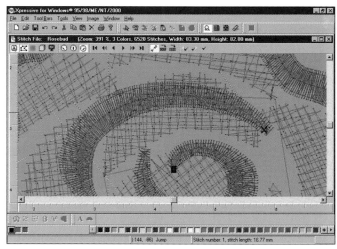

*Stitch points in Elna software.*

All digitized designs have stitch points. The points are used to identify the boundaries or design stitches. These points are also known as beads, nodes, or anchor points and can be viewed on-screen in digitizing software. The manual placement of points around a graphic image forms a manually digitized design.

> Always use the "zoom" function when manually digitizing over a graphic image. This will help you to create detailed professional looking embroidery.
>
> **— Regena Carlevaro**

Some software packages offer curved or straight-line formation with shortcut keystrokes or mouse clicks. Some offer easy recognition of lines being straight or curved by the shape of the point. Use the minimum number of points to define an area when manually digitizing a design.

Points in some digitizing programs are colored for identification and others have an initial. Get to know the symbols that make up a design on-screen, such as the start point, the stop point, color change, etc.

---

*A NOTE FROM JEANINE:*

For manual digitizing, only digitize the points needed to create an object. Too many points can cause a design to not run smoothly or be a bit rough around the edges.

---

### Free-Motion Digitizing

Digitizing with randomly placed stitch points and, loose-fill stitches is a fun alternative to digitizing with a graphic image. Start with a new file in digitizing software and a shape. Manually place stitch points to form random stitches. Loosen the stitch density to form a light and airy design. Add additional layers to blend thread colors.

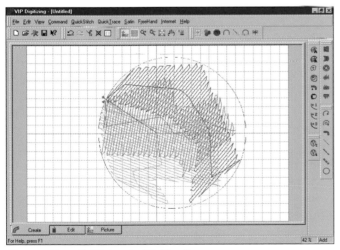

*Free-motion digitizing in Pfaff software.*

With loosely laid stitches, underlay is not necessary. Make the necessary color stops, color changes, and lock stitches to change thread colors. Change the direction of the stitching, or copy and mirror areas of stitching within the design area. Use all the stitches available in the digitizing software as no two designs will be the same.

### Saving

Some software packages have several file formats assigned to different stages of the digitizing process. The most common are outline and stitch file formats. One saves the graphic image outline and changes can be made to the file. The other saves the stitches and minimal changes can be made to the file.

---

Safety First! As soon as you have started a new design, click on the "disk" icon and "save" your design. After a couple of sections, click on the "Disk" icon again to update your file. This will prevent the loss of information should you encounter a power surge, loss of electricity, or an accidental mishap with the computer.

*– Robert Decker*

---

For best results, limit file format names to eight characters plus the appropriate three-letter extension. Some software packages and embroidery machines have difficulty recognizing design names longer than eight characters. Even though computers will recognize longer filenames, individual embroidery software packages or machines may not—especially if the products being used are older.

### Importing to Digitizing Software

Some digitizing software can import stock embroidery designs. If a stock design needs changes, determine if your digitizing program can import the design to make changes. Once the design is in your digitizing software, changes to underlay, density, size, and stitch length may be possible. If the design is too dense, change the density or enlarge the design without changing the stitch count. If the design is not appropriately sized, enlarge it in a digitizing or sizing program. Depending on the software, a multitude of changes can be made to a stock design in digitizing software.

# An Exercise in Digitizing

A circle is the best graphic image to experiment using digitizing techniques.

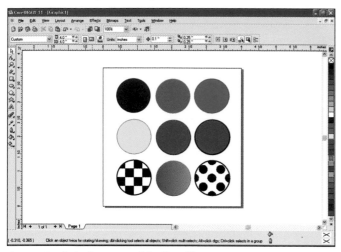

*A group of circles created in CorelDraw.*

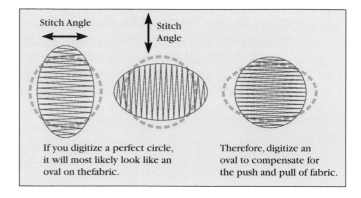

If you digitize a perfect circle, it will most likely look like an oval on the fabric.

Therefore, digitize an oval to compensate for the push and pull of fabric.

1.  Create a circle or a group of circles in a graphic art software program. Flood the circles with a color and a black outline. Save the images as a recognizable filename (.BMP, .WMF, .JPG). Or, create a circle directly in your digitizing software, if possible.

2.  Load the image into your digitizing software. Next, to automatically digitize the circle, click on the image and create stitches. Or, manually create stitches by adding stitch points to the circle perimeter. To form curved edges, it may be necessary to hold down the "shift" or "CTRL" buttons on the keyboard while assigning the stitch points. Then, add underlay, set the fill stitches, and the outline type.

3.  Once the circle is completely digitized and looks perfect on screen, transfer the design to the embroidery machine, hoop the fabric with the appropriate stabilizer, and embroider the circle.

4.  To determine if the underlay stitches, pull compensation, or density need adjustments, look at the test-stitch sample. Is the shape distorted? More underlay and pull compensation may be required to hold the shape. Are the edges of the circle jagged or is the fabric showing through the stitches? More density may be needed to keep the stitches tighter.

5.  Make the necessary adjustments in the software. Skew the design on-screen if necessary to make the correct adjustments. Test-stitch the design again.

6.  Experiment by embroidering circles onto a variety of fabrics, using multiple fill patterns and stitch angles. Notice how the design stitches differently on assorted fabrics. Adjust the pull compensation, density, underlay stitches, stabilizer, and stitch length if necessary. Fix all the problems and test-stitch again. Keep a notebook of "before" and "after" test-stitch samples with detailed information for future reference.

7.  Next, create the circle as an appliqué, then with an assortment of edge finishes. Experiment with shading—adding depth and texture to the circle. Make a gradient circle using light to dark thread colors.

8.  Use the graphic images on the CD-ROM to experiment with a wide variety of digitizing exercises.

**HINT:** When digitizing the circle, consider the fabric grain and the stitch angle. The greater stretch is usually from selvedge to selvedge. The least amount of stretch is from cut edge to cut edge. Fabric also has stretch in both diagonal directions, known as the "bias." Take the fabric stretch into consideration when digitizing a design. On some fabrics, stitches could imbed into the fabric depending on the stitch angle. For denim, do not digitize stitches in the fabric diagonal grooves. Fills should stitch in the least stretchy fabric direction with a cut-away stabilizer and topping.

# Design Digitizing Properties

Use these properties to get you started digitizing basic shapes and designs with embroidery techniques.

## Traditional Appliqué

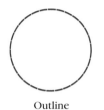  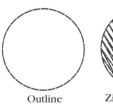

Outline (stop)  Zigzag Underlay  3-4mm Satin Stitches

## Fills

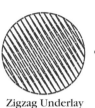 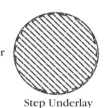

Outline  Zigzag Underlay  or  Step Underlay

Fill Stitches

## Blanket Stitch Appliqué

 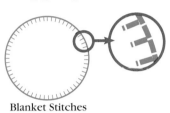

Outline (stop)  Blanket Stitches

## Small Leaves and Flower Petals

Fill Stitches  3-Step Zigzag Underlay  Satin Stitches  or

## Cutwork

Outline (stop)  Zigzag Underlay  Satin Stitches

## Lettering Options

  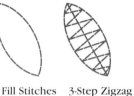

Outline  Zigzag Underlay (optional for all)  Satin Stitches

Double Outline  Satin Stitches

Triple Outline  Satin Stitches

## Satin Column/Fill

Outline  3-Step Zigzag Underlay in larger areas  Satin/Fill Stitches

## Dimensional

Always digitize free-standing dimensional designs with a satin stitch along the edge.

Fill Stitches  Zigzag Underlay  Satin Stitches

# Chapter 6
# Specialty Software

There are many specialty software packages available to make the embroidery process easy and fun. From cross stitch software that duplicates the look of handwork to individual density, sizing and cataloging software packages, the selection of specialty software is expanding exponentially.

### A NOTE FROM JEANINE:

Most embroidery software has overlapping features and capabilities. Some individual software may have more than one task. For example, lettering software may have customizing capabilities. Look for multiple capabilities within each software package you own.

*An assortment of embroidery software.*

---

## Design Cataloging

### What's Design Cataloging?

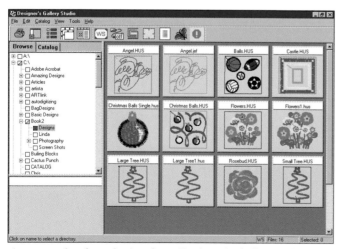

*An example of cataloging from Designer's Gallery software.*

Organizing designs on a computer hard-drive is one way to catalog. Another is to use binders of hard-copy information, such a design print outs,

templates, and test-stitch samples. Cataloging software helps make this process easy. Use it to locate designs on a computer, print design templates, convert designs from one file format to another, and so much more. Cataloging software can be bundled within larger embroidery programs or available separately from independent software or machine manufacturers.

Cataloging can be performed with software packages that may have some of these key features:

- Adds design perimeter baste
- Assists with design and image downloads
- Automatic folder tree
- Single or batch design conversion
- Browse designs and graphics on the computer
- Converts digitized designs to bitmaps for re-digitizing
- Creates a second file when making changes to original

- Creates design cataloging categories and sub-categories
- Creates design notes
- Cross reference designs
- Drag and drop designs into file cataloging categories
- File management functions: view, rename, sort, copy, more
- Fixes corrupt design files
- Helps locate designs on computer
- Image conversion from vector to bitmap file format
- Opens designs directly into embroidery software
- Pictorial catalog—produces a design slide show
- Print design catalog and small design images
- View and print folders and templates with design details
- Zips and Unzips designs

> Create several folders for design organization. When downloading designs from the Internet, place them in the folders by company or design type. This will make locating designs much easier.
> **—Annette Bailey**

## Getting Organized

Cataloging software works best on an organized computer. With the large assortment of designs available for sale or for free, it is helpful to keep track of the designs for easy access and use. Think of a computer as a filing cabinet containing folders (the main operating system plus your embroidery software, designs, tutorials, graphic images, and documents).

When adding software, designs, and hardware to your computer, locate where files are being saved on the computer. Understanding how a computer filing system works and being able to manually select the destination file folder will ultimately provide a more organized computer.

A computer has an operating system—either Macintosh- or Windows-based. It is important to know how to create folders and sub-folders. Refer to the computer user's guide or "Help" menu functions when in doubt. A computer comes standard with preset folders for the system. The remaining hard-drive space is available for storing your files and information.

To get started, create a design filing system on paper. Then, create the same file folders and sub-folders on the computer using cataloging software.

In the beginning, it may be more helpful to purchase several three-ring binders, a three-hole punch, and tab dividers. When obtaining a new design, print out a template, three-hole punch the page, and add it to the binder. Note the location on the page where the design can be found in the computer hard-drive. Starting with a hard-copy organizing system will help you work through a system for your computer.

## Design Organization

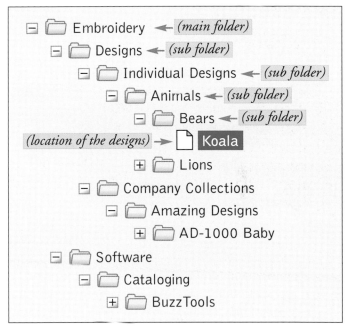

To start, use one main computer folder for all your embroidery needs. Start with a folder entitled "Embroidery." Next, create these five sub-folders:

- Designs
- Software
- Tutorials
- Graphic Images
- Documents

Once these folders are created, start creating sub-folders in each folder for the design file types used regularly. If designs are currently on the computer, create all the applicable folders and sub-folder. Then, move designs to the appropriate folders. For your convenience, a listing of design categories for a computer design filing system is located in Appendix II starting on page 114.

Organize design packs by manufacturer and individual designs by theme. Keep design packs bundled together in numeric order. Or, consider breaking down the packaging to fit into binders and disk carrying cases. With today's technology there are a variety of ways to store information—both on the computer and with containers in a variety of sizes.

O nce you have designs organized into categories on a computer, you can easily locate them. Download files directly to the folder it belongs—download a digitized cat to a "Cats" folder, a digitized dog to a "Dogs" folder, etc. Another technique is to first download to a folder named "Downloads." Then, unzip or convert the files, if necessary, to place the designs into appropriate folders. Unzipping can be accomplished with a specialty file compression utility, or some computers can unzip files with the operating systems. However, specialty cataloging software can usually unzip and convert all in one program.

*— Lisa Shaw*

## Locating Folders

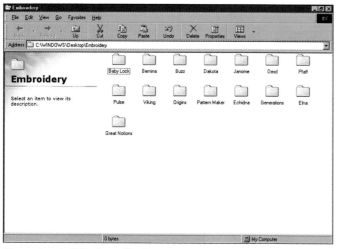

*Browsing in Windows Explorer.*

Choose your own file destination when downloading, installing, or saving designs or software to a computer. When downloading or installing onto a computer, a dialog box will ask for the file destination. Browse through the computer filing system to locate the "Embroidery Designs" or "Embroidery Software" folder, and then find the sub-file folders of the final destination. When saving or transferring designs from a disk to the computer, copy the files directly to the final destination.

I like to save my purchased designs by "designer" with subfolders for each collection/theme. Each time I purchase a new collection from the "designer" I create a folder with the collection's name and copy my newly purchased treasures to this folder. This way, I know where I got a specific design and if I'm looking for a coordinating design, I can check the "designer's" Web site first.

*— Lisa Shaw*

## Copyright Laws

Adhere to the copyright laws when downloading, saving, and storing designs. Obtain designs legally. Do not share, copy, sell, or trade embroidery designs. When downloading free designs from the Internet, keep a notebook or log where the designs are available should a friend want to obtain the same design. Send friends to the Web site where the free design is available to download their own copy. It is illegal to copy a design and send it to a friend—even if the design was free—this action violates the copyright laws. The only person who can distribute designs is the originating company or individual.

## Design Conversion

Designs can be converted to a host of file formats using cataloging software. To do so, select the design image and choose the appropriate Menu button for the conversion. Follow the guided steps through the process to convert the design to the appropriate file format. For more information on design conversion, refer to page 80.

## Using Zipped Files

A "zipped" file has compressed data and is used to transfer stitch information across the Internet. Most cataloging software can open and access the contents of compressed design files by uncompressing the data. Use cataloging software to open and save the contents of compressed design files to your computer, and then add designs to your "filing system."

## Printing Design Information

It is possible to print an assortment of information from cataloging software. A worksheet containing the actual design size, design thread colors, and size information can be printed as well as thumbnail images of designs saved in folders on the computer. Use the software's printing feature to keep hard copies of designs in binders for easy reference.

 **A NOTE FROM JEANINE:**

Often PDF (portable document format) files on the design disks or within software may include information such as thread colors, templates, helpful hints, tutorials, etc. Print the PDF files and keep the pages with the design information for future reference.

## Design Notes

Some software packages can keep notes about designs. This function is helpful to remember important design information, such as the thread, needle, and stabilizer to use, the fabric the design is intended for, and other pertinent information.

**A NOTE FROM JEANINE:**

Keep notes on designs for sharing design originating Web sites or store information with friends. Keep the manufacturer, Internet address, or disk pack information in the design notes, too.

## A Backup System

Always keep a backup system of designs should something happen to your computer. Consider purchasing an external hard-drive where data can be stored regularly or when changes are made to design files. Or, consider backing up files onto disks. In addition to re-writeable CD-ROMS and floppy disks, there are several disks available for housing large volumes of data, such as Zip disks. Look for the most up-to-date way of backing up and storing data at a local computer or office supply store.

When a large number of designs have been obtained, saving designs on multiple disks is

*Design file backup disks.*

possible. Use a multitude of disks with a variety of themes. Organize the disks by theme to make sure all the information will fit onto the disks. If a disk runs out of room, it will be necessary to break the information into multiple disks, such as Volume 1, 2, etc. Keeping a hard-copy back-up of design information can also be effective for cataloging a large assortment of designs.

For permanent design storage, one-time writeable CD-ROM disks are ideal. However, continual updates to file folders and category folders may make this method inefficient. Instead consider a storage method that allows multiple updates. The easiest way to save a back-up of design files is with an external hard-drive with volume capacity and a USB port connection. Copy the "Embroidery" folder with all the sub-folders and files from the hard-drive to the external hard-drive. Unplug the device when not in use.

Some people like to store designs on floppies, Zip disks, or writeable CD-ROMS. If you don't have an organizing "system" for storing designs, you'll have a hard time locating specific designs. If you have a cataloging software program, print a summary of a design storage disk with the filename and thumbnails (small image) of designs. Put the printout and the storage unit (floppy) into a sheet protector and then into a binder. This is the best way to create a visual Table of Contents of the files on the diskette.

*— Lisa Shaw*

# Lettering

The addition of words, letters, or sayings to embroidery is a fun way to express creativity.

*Lettering in Viking software.*

## What's Lettering?

Lettering is the creation of alphabetic characters, numbers, or words for embroidery. Lettering can be performed with software packages that may have some of these key features:

- Above and reverse arching
- Built-in borders and shapes
- Change height and width of letters
- Change letter density
- Change thread colors
- Import digitized fonts
- Italicize letters
- Kerning—Auto and manual
- Left, right and center justification
- Lettering and monogram creation
- Multiple baselines
- Multiple fonts per line
- Multiple line text
- Nearest point letter joining
- Skew lettering
- Underlay options
- Word shaping: Arch, bridging, vertical, etc.

> Y ou can easily use letters to create wonderful designs just by resizing, rotating, mirroring and putting more than one or two letters together to make a pleasing design.
>
> *— Nicky Bookout*

Some software can create lettering from computer True-Type fonts. Others can only set up customized words, letters or monograms. It is important to treat each letter as an individual design with the proper underlay, stitch density, pull compensation, and stabilization.

## Playing with Words

*Lettering with a Cactus Punch design.*

Lettering can add pizzazz to any design especially when combined with stock embroidery designs to create playful sayings. To get started, Appendix III on page 116 has a multitude of clever sayings that can be used alone or with stock embroidery designs. Combine the sayings with designs in lettering, customizing, automatic digitizing, or other letter creation software.

## Stitches

For small- to medium-size lettering, satin stitches are commonly used. For best results, use a 6-9mm stitch width maximum for satins. For larger lettering, use fill stitches. Most embroidery machines speed up and slow down with the stitch length. Smaller stitches will provide a faster embroidered design.

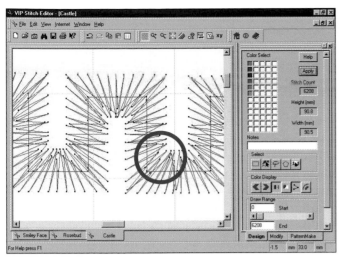

*The shorten stitches feature in Pfaff software.*

The rounding or turning of corners in lettering can be bulky with an increased number of stitches in a smaller area. Use a "shorten stitches" feature that shortens a random number of stitches within an inner corner or curve. Some stitches will remain longer and others will be shortened to compensate for the number of stitch points hitting the small area of a curve or corner.

### Underlay

Using underlay stitches in lettering is vitally important to the outcome of smoothly embroidered letters and numbers. There are three types of underlay stitches for lettering—an outline with a zigzag, a center run with a zigzag, or a single center run for small, narrow lettering. Check to make sure that underlay stitches are beneath lettering top stitches. Some lettering software provides choices for underlay. Choose one suitable for the fabric and style of lettering.

### Small Lettering

For best results, embroider lettering with a smaller needle and a thinner thread (70/10 or 65/9 size needle and 50- to 60-weight thread). Slow the machine speed to allow the machine time to embroider the stitches. Small lettering should only be used on appropriate fabric. Small lettering on the wrong fabric will bury into the fabric or the needle will deflect on the fibers causing improperly stitched embroidery.

To aid in the stitching of small lettering, a textured or solid base of fill stitches can be used to hold down the fabric nap. This technique will prevent small lettering from imbedding into fabric.

To digitize the lettering "patch," determine the finished size of the lettering. Create a shape similar

to the lettering—oval, square, rectangle or a harmonious shape. Fill the shape with underlay appropriate for the fabric and complex fill with an angle opposite to the lettering angle. Combine the lettering with the shape fill in software and send the design to the embroidery machine.

### Baselines

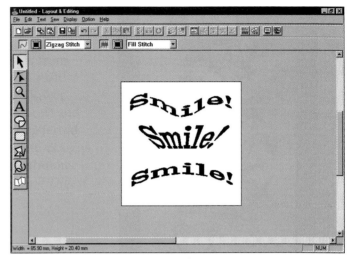

*Baseline examples in Brother software.*

Letters can be manipulated to form a variety of shapes—arch, bridge, vertical, straight line, and curved. The baseline is the path in which lettering is laid. Letters can be shaped and skewed into a variety of baselines to add interest to words. The baseline can be adjusted to meet your personal preference or surround a digitized design.

Most software allows the formation of words or letters with a multitude of baseline options. Once a baseline is chosen, it is possible to change. When changing baselines before the embroidery process, make sure the software also compensates by changing the stitch lengths and underlay stitches. The stitch count of the lettering motif should change as the baseline changes and the letters are being skewed.

### Kerning

Kerning is the space between the letters. Some software has automatic kerning, while others have manual placement. As lettering is placed into software, letters can vary in width. A smaller letter placed next to a large letter should not have even spacing. Letters should be proportionately spaced to avoid larger or smaller gaps.

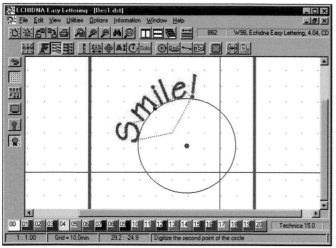

*A kerning example in Echidna Easy Lettering software.*

A cursive string of letters may be perfectly placed on a straight baseline, but the same string of letters on a curve may fall out alignment. Be sure that cursive letters stay connected during any baseline adjustment.

> I like to make the inside of my garments as pretty as the outside. I often take a simple outline (or True-Type Font images that are not letters, such as "Wingdings") and embroider these randomly all over the front and back lining areas.
>
> **– Penny Muncaster-Jewell**

# Cross Stitch

With a computer and specialty software, hand charted cross stitch can be automated for embroidery machine stitching.

## What's Cross Stitch?

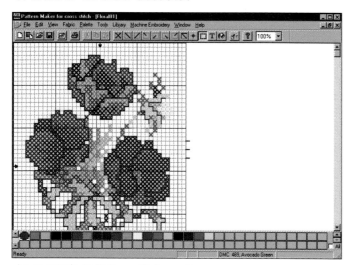

*An example in Pattern Maker software.*

A cross stitch forms an "X" on fabric. Most cross stitch designs are composed "X" stitches combined with straight backstitches to outline the design features.

Cross stitch designs can be created with software packages that may have some of these key features:

- Automatic, semi-automatic, and manual digitizing
- Automatic symbol recognition
- Blend thread colors
- Combine designs

- Create multi-hoop designs
- Design conversion
- Flood fill
- Hoop size selection
- Image adjustment
- Produces a backstitch outline
- Provides alignment stitches for split designs
- Scan images directly into software
- Split designs

> Look for cross stitch software that can create backstitch outlines. While most cross stitch software can import graphic images and automatically generate cross stitches, not all can generate backstitch outlines. For best results, import a graphic image into cross stitch software. Then, manually chart the design stitch-by-stitch over the image.
>
> **– Donna Vermillion Giampa**

Cross stitch software is generally user friendly. Some feature automatic creation of cross stitch designs while others use semi-automatic or manual functions. Use the hints and tips, found in Chapter 5—Digitizing, to create cross stitch designs. Open or import a graphic image, automatically or manually assign stitches to the image. Most cross stitch software has an on-screen grid set up for each "X" to be placed in the graphic image. Click the on-screen thread colors with the mouse and click on the grid boxes in the graphic image to color the design. Use portions of the "X" to eliminate jagged edges near the design boundaries.

It may be possible to open or import digitized cross stitch designs into software for editing. Depending on the software, design source, and file format, it may be possible to resize, edit stitches, and perform color changes and sorts. Refer to the owner's manual to determine the file formats that can be opened or imported into your cross stitch software.

> **C**ross stitch designs can usually be safely enlarged or reduced 10 percent without changing the basic stitch quality. I would suggest test stitching a small portion of the design to verify the quality of the re-sized stitches. If the design is reduced and the stitches are not clear and even, try a thinner thread. If the design is enlarged and the thread coverage appears "sparse," use a thicker thread. Or, stitch each color twice to obtain better thread coverage.
>
> *– Donna Vermillion Giampa*

## Fabrics

The best fabric to use for cross stitch is one with an open, even weave, such as linen, Aida cloth (traditional cross stitch fabric), or cotton. If Aida cloth is used, make sure the fabric is on the straight of grain in the hoop. Embroidery on tightly woven fabrics can form puckers surrounding the stitches. Choose fabrics that have some breathing room in the weave to form stitches.

> **S**low down your embroidery machine— your stitches will be neater! Then, loosen the top tension slightly—your cross stitches will be a little fuller with less fabric distortion.
>
> *– Donna Vermillion Giampa*

## Stitches

Variations of the "X" are used to form cross stitch designs. From the full cross stitch to a quarter cross stitch, depending on where the "X" falls in the graphic image will determine what variation to use.

*An example of a cross stitch project from Vermillion Stitchery*

### Backstitches

Backstitches are used last to outline and highlight design areas. Stitch the backstitches first to determine the design size and areas where the "X" stitches will form. The outline can also hold the fabric and stabilizer layers together to ensure successful embroidery results.

> **C**ross stitch designs have different color stops for the stitches and for the backstitches (the outlining stitches). For a crisp, clean design, you'll want the backstitches to embroider after all the cross stitches are complete. For best results when using customizing software to sort colors, only combine colors that are the same stitch type. For example, combine all the same color cross stitches together, and then all the same color backstitches. Avoid using any automatic sorting process. The automatic color sorting processes will more than likely combine the cross stitches and the backstitches, "muddying up" your final stitch out.
>
> *– Donna Vermillion Giampa*

### Jump Stitches

Cross stitch designs have more jump stitches than a standard embroidery design. Therefore, it is important to trim often. It is not advisable to embroider over jump stitches as it may render the stitches permanent or obstruct the stitching of other thread colors.

## Embroidery Supplies

The supplies for cross stitch rarely change as the fabric is usually woven and the designs are densely covered with stitches.

### Needle and Thread Choices

For best results, use a 75/11 embroidery needle with 50- or 60-weight cotton thread to imitate the look of hand stitches. Follow color suggestions from the design manufacturer for the order of thread colors, as each embroidery machine translates embroidery thread colors differently. When embroidering with cotton thread, be sure to keep the machine clean of lint. Stop and clean the machine often to avoid any embroidery problems.

> T o obtain embroidery results that most closely resemble hand cross stitch, use cotton embroidery thread. This type of thread has less sheen than rayon or polyester, therefore providing a softer look and feel to your finished project.
> **– Donna Vermillion Giampa**

### Stabilizers

Use minimal stabilization behind fabric when embroidering cross stitch designs. Embroider using a heavier stabilizer for large hoops and a lighter stabilizer for smaller hoops.

The weight of the fabric, the size of the stitches, and the weight of the thread all impact the stabilizer requirements. For most standard cross stitch designs, use a medium-weight tear-away stabilizer in the hoop with another layer placed between the bed of the machine and the hoop. An adhesive tear-away stabilizer in the hoop can also be used with successful results.

Hoop the medium-weight stabilizer, spray the stabilizer with adhesive, and secure the fabric to the hoop (noting fabric grain alignment). Then, attach the hoop to the machine and slide a piece of tear-away under the hoop. If your machine has a perimeter baste feature, use this basting stitch to hold all

the layers together. Lower the top thread tension and slow the machine speed for best cross stitch embroidery results.

## Splitting Designs

The number of thread colors in a cross stitch design is higher than in a standard embroidery design. Depending on the embroidery machine, a cross stitch design may require stitching in several segments, as there may be more thread color changes than an embroidery machine can stitch in one segment.

It will be necessary to split design files when an embroidery machine has color stop limitations, usually between 12-15 colors. The design file must be split into two or more files depending on the colors in the design and limitations of the machine. Many professional design manufacturers know what machines have these limitations and will provide the adequate number of files for the file format. It is important to load all the files onto your embroidery machine to make the design complete. Immediately after embroidering part one of the design, embroider part two as if continuing with the next color. Be sure to note the exact position of the needle start position, if alterations were made to the position of the design for the stitching of step one.

*An example of a cross stitch project from Elna.*

# Other Software

There are a multitude of individual software packages available to help make the embroidery process easier. Look for new specialty software at your local embroidery machine dealer. Always choose software based on the embroidery requirements you desire.

## Density Editor

Changing the stitch density of a design can make it embroider better. This type of software analyzes and adjusts the stitch density for smoother embroidered designs with less stabilization.

## Color Editor

The editing of thread colors, including the stitching order, is made easy with type of software. Adding, deleting, or changing color stops in addition to viewing and watching a design embroider on-screen is this software's specialty.

## Fancy Fills Editor

Use this software to add texture to designs by adding or changing fill patterns. When converting designs from one file format to another, sometimes the fill stitch patterns are eliminated. Use this type of software to add fill stitch patterns to designs.

> Use a quick-fill stitch-changing program for adding dimension and texture to your embroidery designs. Remember—you don't need to change all the elements of a design into a patterned fill. Try changing different sections of the design to see what looks best. With a realistic view feature, it's easy to see what the stitched design will look like.
>
> *– Nancy Zieman*

## Picture Stitch

This software can assign stitches to a photographic image. The stitches can be cross stitches, single stitches in varying lengths, or stippling stitches to reproduce the photograph with thread. Open fabric and a multitude of thread colors define the embroidery image.

*Angel design from the CD-ROM.*

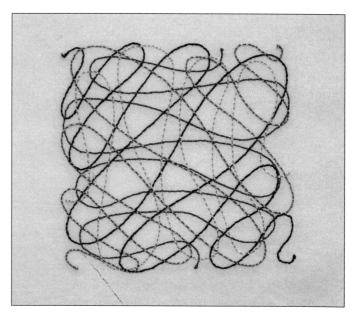

*Squiggle design from the CD-ROM.*

# Chapter 7
# Design File Format Conversion

The conversion of designs from one file format to another is possible with embroidery software, specialty software, or conversion boxes. But, the ability to convert designs comes with a large responsibility. Be honest and follow the copyright laws. The ability to convert decorative designs is for those who own more than one embroidery machine and need a variety of file formats extensions, for those who want to convert free designs to embroider on their embroidery machine, or for those who use other embroidery machine manufacturer's designs.

> It is important to realize that when you purchase embroidery designs, you must know how to transfer those files to your machine. This process requires some knowledge of your embroidery machine and the software needed to transfer the files. Each embroidery machine varies in its requirements, so call or visit your dealer to learn what you need to know.
>
> — *Donna Vermillion Giampa*

## Copyright Laws

The ability to convert designs from one file format to another is for personal use only and not for sharing purchased, free designs, or memory cards. Respect the copyright laws. It protects designers and thereby assures a steady supply of original designs with high-quality digitizing and standards.

## Downloading Designs

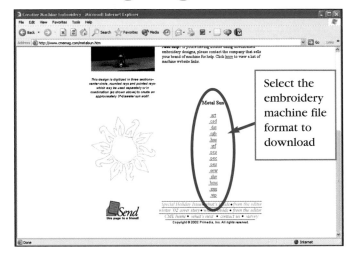

*Downloading a design from **www.cmemag.com** Web site.*

Designs can be downloaded from Internet Web sites. A listing of the available file format extensions as usually listed. If decorative designs are not available in your particular machine file format, purchase designs in the original digitizing software file format. Then, import the designs into your software and save designs in your embroidery file format. If your software can open, import, and export most file formats, get to know the formats

Knowing the file formats your software can utilize will make the downloading process much easier.

When saving a file to your computer hard-drive, a dialog box will initiate a prompt for the location where the file is to be saved. Follow the prompts to locate a "home" for files on your hard-drive.

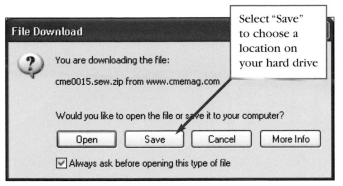

*A standard File Download Dialog Box.*

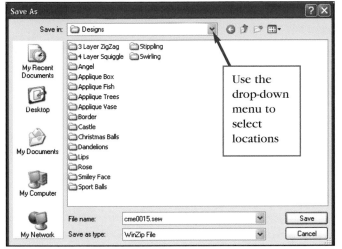

*Browse your computer hard drive for a location to save the design.*

Most files downloaded from a Web site are compressed in a ZIP or EXE file to download faster and not lose important stitch data during the transfer process. There are a variety of ways to uncompress files—EXE files do not require any additional software; a ZIP file requires specific software to extract the files.

*The contents of a zipped file.*

Either method is fine and is simple to operate from the dialog box prompts. Understand where downloaded files will be saved. Download designs directly to your computer hard drive. Once the files are saved, make your back-up copies—whether on CD, disk, or external hard-drive.

## Conversion Process

When converting designs from one file format to another, start with the original file format (native file format) if possible. The native file format contains the original specifications created from the digitizing software and designs will convert with more accuracy.

For best results, keep a copy of designs in the original format, and then convert to your embroidery machine file format using another filename. Keep the original, and then "Save As" to create a copy. Save all original foreign file formats in one location. Then, should another embroidery machine with a different file format be purchased or a problem with the converted file arise, the copy provides a back-up for future use.

Overall conversion success will be best from the original file—multiple conversions from format to format can cause design degradation and lost stitches in the translation. This design degradation can lead to embroidery frustration when converting from non-original formats. If a design is not properly transferred over the Internet, degradation can occur and cause embroidery problems. For best results, convert from the original file format and compress designs for transfer over the Internet.

Professionally digitized designs have been converted and tested. Therefore, simply install, download, or save the appropriate machine-specific file format extension to the computer hard-drive.

### Limited File Format Availability

When designs are available in limited file formats, the design may be too large for the file format or the digitizer could not provide all the file formats. First, check the design size. If the size is larger than 4" square, the design is only compatible with those embroidery machines that can stitch larger designs. Then, check with the digitizing individual or company. Some digitizing software programs have limited file format saving capabilities. If this is the case, convert the design in your software. Purchase or download the original file format (if applicable) or a commercial file format, such as DST.

Determine other file formats that are compatible with your embroidery equipment. For example, some software packages can open, import, or convert using the HUS format with the least amount of design degradation. This means that if a design is not available in your machine file format, download another and convert it to your machine-specific file format. The only way to test other machine brand file formats is to open, import, or convert a variety of files and test-stitch.

If a design is not available in your format and your embroidery software cannot open or import the foreign file formats, then purchase conversion software, made specifically for translating stitch files. Some software packages that specialize in the conversion of embroidery file formats may have other features, such as cataloging and organizing embroidery designs, unzipping multiple files, and batch file format conversions. Look for conversion software than works with your embroidery equipment.

### Fancy Fills and Specialty Stitches

Specialty stitches created in one file format may not translate well to another embroidery machine or software. The file may convert in software, but how well an embroidery machine reads the stitch data cannot be anticipated. It is important to download or digitize designs in simple stitches (without fancy fills) for use with all embroidery machines. If you are digitizing for your personal use and with software that is specific for your embroidery equipment, then digitize fancifully, as your embroidery machine will be able to read and stitch the decorative stitches.

### Design File Formats

Embroidery machine manufacturers have propriety file format extensions assigned to help their machines recognize stitch commands. The file formats are the three-letter extensions found at the end of a filename and are unique to the embroidery machine or software.

Conversion software must be programmed to recognize the file format stitch commands. The conversion process includes the translation of unique design properties so that the applicable software or embroidery machine can recognize the commands. If the conversion of designs is not accurate, design degradation or error messages will occur. It is common to discover that some software cannot convert, recognize, import or open designs in other file formats.

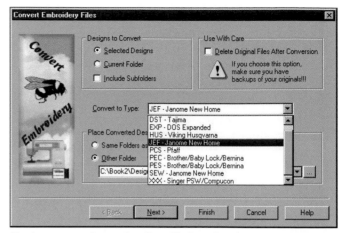

*Design conversion using BuzzTools software.*

With the large number of embroidery file formats, there is not one software package that can convert every embroidery machine file format. In some cases, it may be necessary to purchase multiple pieces of software. Some machine file formats can only be recognized with the proper product specific software.

With more than 30 embroidery machine or software file formats, it is important to understand the limitations of embroidery software and equipment. For example, get to know the maximum size design your embroidery machine can embroider. If the file format extension is limited to 4" square designs, it will not be possible to utilize larger designs without modification, such as resizing, design splitting, or using a specialty hoop.

Below is a listing of home embroidery file formats. These are the most commonly found formats that can be opened or imported into home embroidery software. For a more complete listing of file formats, refer to Appendix I on page 112.

### Commonly Used File Formats

| | |
|---|---|
| BMP | Windows Bitmap |
| ART | Bernina |
| CSD | POEM, Singer EU, Viking Huskygram |
| DST | Tajima (Commercial) |
| EMD | Elna (Exquisite), Singer (XL-5000) |
| HUS | Husqvarna Viking, Pfaff (2140) |
| JEF | Janome (10000) |
| PCM | Pfaff – MAC (7570 and earlier models) |
| PCS | Pfaff – Windows (7570 and earlier models) |
| PES | Baby Lock, Bernina (Deco), Brother, Simplicity, White |
| PHC | Baby Lock (Ellageo), Brother (2000 series) |

| SEW | Elna (CE20 and earlier models), Janome (9000 and earlier models), Kenmore |
| SHV | Husqvarna Viking (Designer 1, 2) via Disk Manager |
| VIP | Husqvarna Viking (Designer 1, 2), Pfaff (2140) |
| XXX | Singer |

## Transfer Media

There is a difference between a conversion box and a read/writer box. A read/writer box is embroidery-machine-specific. The box is used to transfer designs from the computer to the read/writer box, or from the read/writer box to the computer. Only designs made specifically for your embroidery machine file format or memory card can be used in this process.

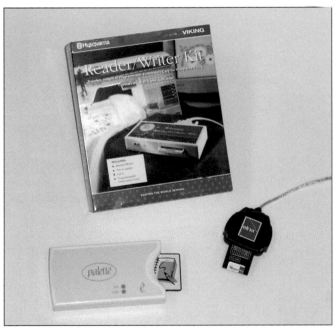

*An assortment of transfer media.*

A conversion box is a universal translator for memory cards. It will assist in the reading and transferring of assorted foreign memory cards to a blank memory card that is embroidery-machine-specific. It will also convert and load embroidery designs installed on a computer from disk packs and the Internet to a blank memory card. A conversion box is perfect for someone who purchases a new machine and needs to convert currently owned memory card designs to another format.

Depending on the use, check with your embroidery machine manufacturer or dealer to determine

the type of device available for your equipment. Both boxes work with stitch-based files—not with graphic images.

As with conversion software, there is not one conversion box that can transfer designs to all embroidery file formats. Conversion boxes are basic. The box allows a design to be read into the manufacturer supplied software, and then saved to a blank memory card that is embroidery-machine compatible. There is no sizing or other specialty features available. Not all memory cards can be read, depending on the conversion box purchased.

> ### A NOTE FROM JEANINE:
>
> It is a user's responsibility to know the limitations for hoop sizes, design colors, design stitch counts, or blank memory cards. Some designs may have more stitches than a blank card or embroidery machine can allow, or may be too large for a hoop size. Understanding these limitations will make the process of design conversion easier to follow.

Some blank brand-specific memory cards will only hold up to 6 designs or a limited number of stitches. Each time the blank memory card is written to through the box, all previous designs on the card are deleted.

Conversion boxes are often used as a first step before purchasing software, as it is an intermediate step for obtaining more designs before the purchase of software. A conversion box will facilitate the embroidery of designs "as is" and is a great way to use embroidery design memory cards from other machine manufacturers.

## Thread Colors

After converting, downloading, or purchasing embroidery designs, be sure to check the accuracy of the colors in your embroidery software. Colors often do not transfer when converting from one format to another because of the color variation sequence between manufacturers. Base color palettes are different among software manufacturers. Only sophisticated design conversion software have these palette color differences built-in so that the colors remain true during the conversion process.

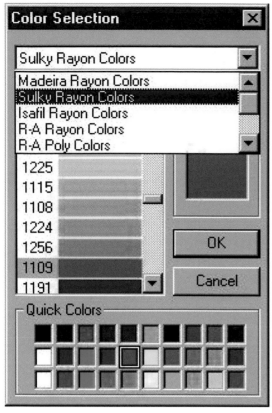

*Color selection in Pfaff software.*

Most professional digitizing companies or individuals provide a color sequence chart with the purchase of designs. Before starting the embroidery process it may be necessary to manually change the design thread colors to the original colors in the embroidery software following the color sequence chart. This step is common and is an important part of the conversion process.

If your software does not have the exact colors from the suggested manufacturer, improvise with colors available in your software. Changing the colors in your software will help ease possible frustration during the embroidery process.

Once the design is downloaded to the embroidery machine, determine if the thread colors transferred according to the color sequence chart. Keep the chart handy during the embroidery of the design. For more information on color changes, see Customizing starting on page 40.

*Rosebud design from the CD-ROM.*

*Vase Flowers design from the CD-ROM.*

# Chapter 8
# Inspirational Embroidery Showcase

## Jody Hooker

Jody is a certified freelance educator for Husqvarna Viking and has extensive experience teaching a variety of sewing techniques. She is a licensed Martha Pullen instructor who travels throughout the United States teaching Sew Beautiful Martha Pullen Schools with Husqvarna Viking. Jody's beautiful sewing talent has been published in Martha's *Sew Beautiful* magazine and has appeared on *America Sews* with Sue Hausmann, and *Sew Young, Sew Fun* TV series.

### *Heirloom Doll Dress*

Embroidered on English netting, this meticulously sewn doll dress features an embroidery design from Martha Pullen's Bullion Roses design disk. To add stability to the fabric, sandwich the netting between two layers of lightweight, water-soluble stabilizer.

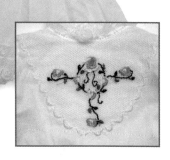

### *Baby Set and Quilt*

This cozy flannel ensemble can make any little one look like a star. Make your own embroidered insertion for the coordinating quilt with the Husqvarna Viking disk from the Patrick Loose collection. The quilt features heirloom techniques on fine cotton batiste inserted into the center of the quilt. Decorative rolled edge serging with variegated thread and decorative lace help to accentuate the embroidered section. As seen in the *Sew Beautiful* magazine.

## Elna USA

The Elna educational team embroidered this wonderful pillow collection.

### Butterfly Pillow

Embroidered butterflies stitched with variegated metallic thread on red silk shantung fabric highlight the butterfly print border fabric. Color-coordinating fringed beading adds the perfect finishing touch. Designs from the Elna embroidery collection.

### Victorian Bed Linens

Lovely are these delicate pillow coverings made from decorator fabric and pure linen. Designs from the *Elna Xquisit Cross Stitch* embroidery collection.

### Delicately Shy Angel

Simply stated is this elegant silk shantung pillow adorned with lace and a single angel motif. Designs from the Elna embroidery collection.

### Plaid Pizzazz

The brightly colored silk plaid fabric paves the way for the subtly embroidered lace motifs on silk taffeta. Designs from the *Elna Xquisit Lace* embroidery collection.

# Annette Bailey

Annette is the editor of *Creative Machine Embroidery* magazine, published by the editors of *Sew News* magazine.

## Wall Décor

Any set of wall frames can become a work of embroidered art. Choose your favorite designs, embroider the motifs on sheer organza, and place behind double panes of glass. For added interest, embroider the motifs in a variety of locations on the fabric for random placement within the frames. To soften the black wrought iron, brown acrylic paint was smoothed randomly over the iron with a knit rag. Any paint color can be used to coordinate with your decor.

## Votive Candle Holders

Create quick gifts using plain glass votive cups as the base. Add a coat of white glue to the outside and sprinkle tiny, glass seed beads to cover it. Or, use specialty bead adhesion tape found at a craft store to secure the beads to the glass. Add an embroidered motif either after beading (snowflake) or before (leaf). The motifs soften and the beads glisten in the candlelight.

## Window Treatment

Your favorite pre-teen girl will love this fun window treatment. It's a simple project that uses three finished bandanas as the curtain. Just embroider motifs on the sides and points. Drape the bandanas over a curtain rod for a quick window treatment or stitch a casing 1" or more at the fold line for insertion of a curtain rod.

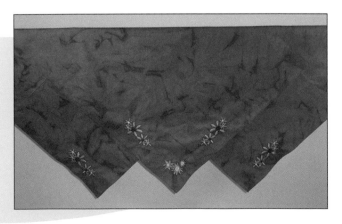

# Cindy Losekamp

Cindy specializes in creative mixed media texture in quilts, wall hangings, wearable art, and sophisticated embroidery designs. Together with her husband, she is the owner of Sew Artfully Yours, a business based on how-to books for Cindy's creative methods of quilting, automatic embroidery, free motion embroidery, stand alone embroidery, and fabric transfer images. Cindy has written 16 books on these subjects including *Secluded Serenity* and *Crochet Crudites*. Here are just a few of her beautiful works of art in the form of wall hangings and purses.

### Secluded Scenic Overlook

This mixed-media scene features a trellis with embroidery designs specifically digitized to hang over the printed fabric. More designs and printed backgrounds were used to finish the project.

### Secluded Cottage

This secluded cottage scene features a printed sky, water, and other objects for the background. Add an assortment of embroidery designs to complete the scene.

# Cindy Losekamp (continued)

### Secluded Lighthouse

This wall hanging features a printable background and detail orientated designs to create this scene. Cindy used inkjet printable backgrounds, printable placement guides, and embroidery designs in several sizes to complete this masterpiece.

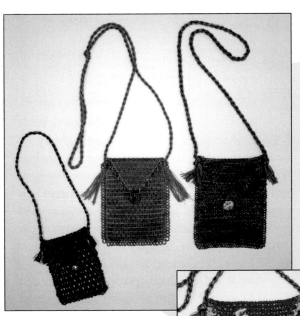

### Crochet Crudités

Affectionately named Crochet Crudités (cru-da-tay), these purses are just a few of the many methods for crocheting using the embroidery machine. Use a 12-weight cotton thread in the needle and the bobbin, a heavyweight water-soluble stabilizer, and a large-eye needle to embroider the meticulously digitized designs.

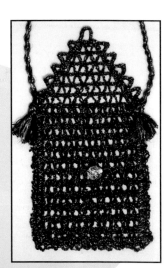

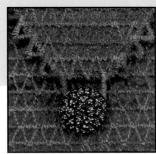

# Janome of America

Your embroidery machine manufacturer works hard to provide you with tools for making embroidery fun. From information online at the company Web site to specialty magazines, look toward embroidery machine manufacturers as a source of information.

### *Pintucked Panel Portrait Dress*

This dress was created by Michele Mishler, a Project Contributor for the *Janome Digest* magazine. Michele's dress was created using a vintage pattern with a pintuck front panel. Using the Memory Craft 10000 and Digitizer 10000 software, Michele was able to modify designs from Memory Card #118 (Border Designs) to accent the pintucks. This sample illustrates that embroidery can be a small accent that complements a larger project.

### *Happycrow*

This child's sweatshirt was also created by Michele Mishler, for the *Janome Digest* magazine. This sample represents the digitizing of a large multi-hoop design and the accurate design placement using the Clothsetter. Michele used her flatbed scanner and the Digitizer 10000 to create this large embroidery design with successful results.

# Janome of America (continued)

### *Fabulous Flowers*

This framed work of art was created by Sheryl Capps, the educational coordinator for Janome. The Customizer 10000 EasyEdit program enables an embroidery design layout to be created in an area that can be expanded to a total of 25" x 33". Sheryl selected a vertical layout to combine designs from Memory Card #130 (Alpine Designs), Memory Card #140 (Butterfly Designs), PC Design Card #1008 (Small Flower Collection), PC Design Card #1010 (Flower Collection) and the MC8000 Design Gallery CD ROM that were transferred from the Memory Craft 10000 to her computer. The designs were stitched in three hoopings to complete this fabulous work of art. For detailed instructions, see the *Janome Digest* Issue #14.

### *A Lesson in Love*

This pillow was created by Regena Carlevaro, the merchandise supervisor for Janome America. A framed picture in a Victorian gift shop originally inspired Regena when she created this wonderful pillow. Combining large lettering, angels from Memory Card #114 *(Angel Designs)* and flowers from PC Design Card #1009 *(Victorian Rose Collection)* in Digitizer 10000 software made it all possible. The individual letters were further combined in Customizer 10000 EasyGigaHoop layout program to enable Regena to stitch this in two hoopings. For detailed instructions, see *Janome Digest* Issue #16.

# Nicky Bookout

Nicky Bookout is a freelance educator with an endless number of creative embroidery ideas!

## *Balsa Basket*

Embroidery on wood! Why not? Thin balsa wood and Viking Card 34 were used to decorate this wooden box purchased from a craft supply store. Use adhesive stabilizer in the hoop to secure the lightweight balsa wood and a lightweight piece of tear-away stabilizer between the hoop and the bed of the machine. With a size 80/12 needle, embroider the design. Gently remove the tear-away stabilizer, but keep the adhesive stabilizer for added strength. Use a rotary cutter to cut the wood to fit the box top and glue the piece in place.

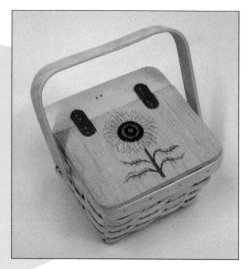

*NOTE:* Stain can be used to color the balsa wood, but apply the stain and allow to dry before the embroidery process.

## *Safari Lamp*

A purchased adhesive lamp base and lampshade were used to create this charming Safari Lamp. Brother Card #30 and little bit of trim embellished the fabric that was cut from the pattern pieces that came with the lamp and shade.

## *Clown Vest*

Here's a first place winner from the Machine Embroidery Enthusiasts Convention, 2001. Fluorescent fabrics and Viking Card #29 were used to create this colorful vest. Nicky loves fluorescent fabrics and her favorite color is lime green. She tries to add this color to just about every project—even if the color is mixed with other thread colors to add a bit of sparkle. You'll be amazed what lime green can do to add a bit of pizzazz to embroidery designs.

# Nicky Bookout (continued)

## Picnic Placesetting

Don't forget about your built-in designs on your embroidery machine, such as this fruit grouping from Husqvarna Viking Designer 1. An assortment of fluorescent fabric colors were used to showcase an assortment of dark thread colors. By embroidering bright color fabrics, your finished projects become more defined. When sewing on dark colors, use more vibrant thread colors—especially on black fabric. Play around with a variety of thread and fabric colors—it's a lot of fun!

## Bug Vest

Nylon screening from a building supply store makes a unique base for the OESD Bugs from Pack #11108. Sandwich the screening between water-soluble stabilizer and embroider the designs. Be sure to soak the screening after completion of the project to dissolve the stabilizer. Use a vest pattern without darts and finish the edges with bias tape for a fun to wear summer vest!

# Nancy Zieman

Nancy Zieman is the president of Nancy's Notions, a mail order business specializing in a wide assortment of sewing and embroidery supplies. She is also the host of *Sewing With Nancy* on PBS and author of large range of books on the subject, including her latest books *Sewing With Nancy's Favorite Hints* and *10•20•30 Minutes to Sew for Your Home* published by Krause Publications.

### Christmas Splendor

Create a mantel scarf using Nancy's *Christmas Splendor* memory card from Amazing Designs. This memory card features designs that capture the tradition and grandeur of the Christmas season, and graceful words that spread the message of peace and love. For a special touch, add subtle radiance with metallic thread.

### Lace Vignettes Dress Scarf

Here's an easy way to re-create the look of antique lace. This charming dresser scarf, Sudberry box insert, and pincushion were made with the Nancy's *Lace Vignettes* memory card from Amazing Designs. For lace-only effect, stitch the lace designs on bridal tulle sandwiched between water-soluble stabilizer. These lovely lace designs are sure to inspire your feminine side.

### Framed Art

These framed landscape scenes, created with the *4-Seasons Landscape Embroidery* Memory Card from Amazing Designs by Nancy and Natalie Sewell, make ideal gifts for your nature loving friends. Select thread colors to reflect their favorite season, then combine design elements to create beautiful indoor retreats, suitable for framing.

# Mary Mulari

Mary Mulari is the author of 14 creative books on the subject of appliqué and the author of *Made for Travel* by Krause Publications. She is known for her creative appliqué techniques and has a multitude of appliqué embroidery designs disks with Amazing Designs, Cactus Punch and Husqvarna Viking.

### Patriotic Handbag

This purse, from Mary's *Accessories with Style* book, features an embroidered flap. The appliqué design was embroidered onto the upper purse flap before the purse was constructed. Embroider a piece of fabric larger than the pattern piece and then cut out pattern from the embroidered fabric. The flag design is from Mary's *Celebrations & Seasons* collection by Amazing Designs.

### Cosmetic Satchel

When appliqué test-stitch samples are stitched on a 9" or larger square of fabric, the fabric can be made into decorative patches or pockets to adorn a multitude of projects. This cosmetic bag, from her *Made for Travel* book, features an embroidered pocket perfect for adding last minute items. Flower design is from Mary's *Favorite Appliqués* collection by Amazing Designs.

### Bag Trio

These trios of purses were featured in the *Designs in Machine Embroidery* magazine, Aug./Sept., 2002 issue. Heavyweight fabric, zippers, decorative stitches and appliqué embroidery adorn these user friendly bags for travel. Mary's creative combination of fabric and thread colors will make these bags easy to find in your suitcase! Designs are from Mary's *Favorite Appliqués* collection by Amazing Designs.

# Linda Griepentrog

Linda Griepentrog is the editor of *Sew News* magazine and the editorial director of *Creative Machine Embroidery* magazine. She loves thinking outside the box for her embroidery adventures.

Never say never is Linda's motto. Yes, you can embroider on metal and create all kinds of things you never thought you could! Why embroider on metal some have asked? Just because you can, and create some really great stuff. These metal items were first showcased in *Creative Machine Embroidery* magazine's Winter '02 issue.

### Framed Flag

Combine metalwork embroidery with a bit of patriotic print fabric for the stars and you have a great home décor item. Stitched with a size 110 needle on copper foil, this Husqvarna Viking disk #27 flag can be displayed with pride.

### Reindeer Ornament

What's better than one needle? How about using three. Use a triple needle to embroider an outline design like this one from Husqvarna Viking disk #27. Be sure to slow the machine speed to prevent needles from breaking and protect your machine base with felt under the metal.

### Framed Quilt Block

Metal flashing accented with an embroidered quilt block (Cactus Punch Quilting 1, Double Pinwheel) adds to any dresser's decor. Choose a frame from the home dec department or make your own, and size your metal embroidery to fit the opening.

*Photos courtesy of* Creative Machine Embroidery *magazine.*

# Linda Griepentrog (continued)

### Clothesline Vest

Linda combined portions of the Husqvarna Viking Design Sampler disk #100, with some dimension—twisted rope and miniature clothespins. Both were suppose to be embroidered sections of the original design but were replaced with the real thing.

### Beetle Bug Vest

Linda owns her second VW bug and chose her favorite fabric—black melton—to showcase this traffic line-up. Colored vinyl topper was used under the Cactus Punch SIG08 cars to prevent the wool surface texture from showing through and distorting the colors.

### All-Over Jacket

The allover design from the Husqvarna Viking design disk #108 used in the jacket panels leave the viewer wondering where one set stops and the other begins. That's the point of proper placement!

# Nancy Cornwell

Nancy Cornwell, affectionately known as the "Polar Princess," has a fun and friendly approach to sewing that appeals to seasoned and novice sewers alike. She has written three best-selling, award-winning books about sewing with fleece, *Adventures With Polarfleece®, More Polarfleece® Adventures,* and *Polar Magic.* Nancy is a sought-after teacher and speaker who loves to share her creative sewing adventures.

### Sampler Tunic

Nancy chose a rich color fleece with a nice hand to create this easy-to-stitch tunic vest. Using the "hidden designs" concept from her *Embroidery Machine Essentials—Fleece Techniques* book, Nancy used the Small Leaf design and proceeded to embroider the leaf designs a variety of ways. She used the satin stitch outline for an accent, the "embossed" look, a bit of texturing, a double-needle outline, and finished with a crisp blunt edge appliqué for center back interest. The laced edge technique completed the wavy rotary cut raw edge. As seen in *Designs in Machine Embroidery* magazine.

### Variegated Scarf

Ombre fleece is a scrumptious double border print that features varying degrees of color intensity. As the perfect embroidery "canvas," Nancy combined the gorgeous coloration of the fleece with complimentary variegated rayon thread to embroider a design from the Husqvarna Viking Sampler disk #100.

### Skeleton Leaf Vest

This vest was featured in Nancy's *Polar Magic* book. She used a variety of leaf motif styles to texturize the fleece. The close stitching lines of the skeleton leaf (crackled veins) embedded into the fleece loft to provide an embossed effect. The leaves outline-stitched with satin or textured stitches contrast the sunken stitches with the fleece loft for subtle texture. For even more textural interest, some leaves used the Trapunto technique for dramatic dimension. The fleece is from David Textiles and the designs are from Nancy's *Adventures With Fleece* disk from Cactus Punch.

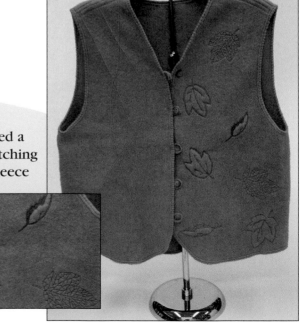

# Mac Berg

"Mac" (as most people call her) has been sewing since about age 10. Although sewing has been a life-long hobby for Mac, her real love is teaching. She is the co-owner of the LakeShore Sewing Depot, in Waukegan, Illinois, and enjoys teaching in her store and for the Original Sewing and Quilt Expo. Mac loves to explore weird and innovative ways to digitize designs for machine embroidery and sewing. Her motto: "If you can cut it with scissors, then why not try to sew it, too!"

### Anti-Mosquito Jacket

This jacket shows that one doesn't always need a stabilizer if the fabric is already stable. Fiberglass screen from the hardware store stretches very little in either direction. Therefore, no stabilizer was needed to embroider the insects. However, the sewing machine needed a finite place to tie a knot—the holes in the screen made it a bit difficult. So, a water-soluble topping was necessary to "fill in" the holes. A 4-thread serger overlock stitch threaded with textured nylon thread was used construct the jacket. Fiberglass screening can be used to sew any project, from tote bags to jackets.

### Pop Tote

I've been having fun experimenting with metal flashing from the hardware store and pop cans burned with a blow torch for appliqué. For this simple tote, I digitized the star for use with a thicker 12-weight cotton thread and adhered double-sided pressure-sensitive fusible web to back of the metal before placing it on the tote fabric. I embroidered the appliqué outline, peeled away the excess metal and then stitched the blanket edge finish. After the appliqué was complete, the double-sided pressure-sensitive fusible web was fused to the tote from the wrong side.

### Delightful Dress

This dress was an exercise in creative placement. Placement of designs in different areas provides a more "expensive boutique" look to items. Look for ideas from ready-to-wear clothing. The dress was also an experiment in using water-soluble stabilizers—experimenting is the only way to learn about stabilizers!

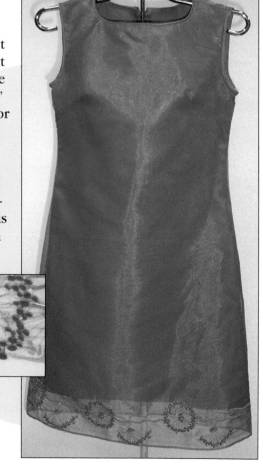

# Bernina Sewing Center of Michigan

*Bernina Deco 600
Built-In Design*

*Bernina Artista
Collection*

*Bernina Collection:
Current® Santas*

*Bernina Artista
Collection*

Marsha Stamps, Judy Marian, Karen Barnowski, and Fran Mills are all employees at the Bernina Sewing Center of Michigan. Their works of embroidery art showcase the education that sewing and embroidery machine dealers all across the country can provide you. Seek the wisdom from your local sewing and embroidery machine dealers to help you learn your embroidery equipment and software.

### Sunflowers Wallhanging

Judy's love for flowers really shows with this easy-to-stitch wall hanging. She embroidered cream colored fabric with designs from OESD and then stitched the squares to color coordinating quilt making fabrics. Substitute the Sunflowers with any designs from your collection.

### Trivet

Ready-to-use clear accessories such as mugs, trivets, soap dispensers and more are great for showcasing your embroidery test-stitch samples. Marsha embroidered a design from the Cactus Punch collection onto cross stitch fabric. The combination of the leaf's skeleton running stitches embroidered with a hand-dyed variegated thread and the textured fabric make this trivet too pretty to cover up with a dish!

### Poinsettia

Karen's holiday table runner is decorated on both ends with appliqué designs from Dalco Home Sew. These easy-to-stitch designs come with pre-cut appliqué pieces. Simply hoop your fabric, stitch the outline, secure the pre-cut appliqué pieces within the stitched outline, and finish the embroidery design. Appliqué made easy!

# Bernina Sewing Center of Michigan (continued)

## Screened Window Wallhanging

Keep fanciful bugs on display in this easy-to-stitch wall hanging idea from OESD. Marsha had fun creating this project with designs embroidered on nylon window screen material from the local building supply store. Backed with quilt fabric that represented clouds and a window, this seasonal wall hanging is sure delight to all that see it at the store.

## Fish Wallhanging

Here's a great project that involves appliqué and some fun quilt fabrics. This wall hanging features appliqué designs from Dalco Home Sew and OESD. Fran had some embroidery fun stitching up this sample for the store.

## Gardening Apron

Marsha loves to keep the embroidery machine stitching just about every moment the store is open. This ready-made gardening apron was the perfect item to showcase Bernina's Karen Rossi Collection.

# Linda Visnaw

Linda Visnaw has been sewing since she was seven and adding embroidery to her capabilities only strengthened the artist in her. She is currently a Freelance Educator for Husqvarna Viking and lives in Lake Havasu City, AZ with her husband. Prior to becoming an educator she managed and was the educational coordinator for a Husqvarna Viking dealer in Michigan. Linda enjoys traveling for Husqvarna Viking and teaching at dealers, and at quilt and craft shows.

## *Abby's Traverse City Cherry Dress and Jacket*

Linda's granddaughter Abby often visits Traverse City (Michigan's Cherry Capital) with her parents, and Linda just knew she'd look adorable in a cute little "Cherry" dress. Using the appliqué cherries from Mary Mulari's Husqvarna Viking card #27 and the Husqvarna Viking Customizing Plus, the designs and lettering were customized for the top of the jumper, the lower edge of the skirt and the left jacket front. Lady Bug buttons were added for just the special touch on the jacket.

## *Embroidered Wool Jumper*

Several hoopings and free motion embroidery were used to create this fabulous dress. On paper, Linda sketched the jumper front and the placement of the flowers from the Husqvarna Viking card #12. She then sketched in the connecting vines and leaves. Chalk was used to mark the flower positions on the front piece of the jumper. Linda chose to embroider the designs in subtle thread colors. With the flowers completed, chalk was again used to draw in the stems and leaves. The same stabilizer used for the embroidery was placed behind the fabric making it easy to complete the stems and leaves using a combination of decorative stitches and free-motion work.

# Penny Muncaster-Jewell

Penny Muncaster-Jewell is a founding member of two Clear Lake Texas area wearables groups. She is an international teacher, speaker, and author of two books on how to digitize. Her third book, entitled *Not Just Another Fish on a T-Shirt*, features one-of-a-kind wearable art.

### Forest Princess

This masterpiece was created using approximately 1,600 embroidered leaves—all made from hand-dyed silk, crystallite organza, specialty fabrics, and lamé cottons. The leaves were digitized in the Brother PE-Design and embroidered using 16 miles of metallic and variegated threads. Each leaf was digitized and embroidered individually, cut out then rejoined to make the base fabric. The base fabric for the cape is made entirely of individual leaves that have been sewn together. Additional leaves have been attached to the base cape fabric to provide movement and a soft rustling sound when worn.

### The Sheer Fall

After a trip to Australia, Penny was determined to make a garment using thread lace created on the embroidery machine. After making 48 sections of thread lace, the sections were connected into strips then cut into flowing curves and rejoined to create the base fabric. Then, a small grid was embroidered over the lace fabric to provide additional stability. Penny digitized and embroidered the leaves to create the finishing edge for the vest. Three larger versions were used to adorn the back. Approximately 16,000 yards of variegated thread were used in this project. It was done almost completely on the embroidery machine, except for connecting the strips of thread lace, seams, and attaching the leaf border.

### The Evening Purse

Using the Brother PE-Design software, Penny created the tiny stippling stitches, French knots and chain stitch outlines. The complete purse was made, lined and constructed entirely on the embroidery machine. She used copper lamé, fused to a lightweight fleece, topped with two layers of tulle, to dull the lamé. The silk fabric in the background was hand dyed by Penny.

# Robert Decker

Robert Decker is the owner of the Decker Design Studio and a freelance educator for Husqvarna Viking. His specialty is teaching embroidery software and digitizing.

### The Pieta

This magnificent large cross stitch design was created using the Husqvarna Viking Cross Stitcher program along with the Husqvarna Viking Stitch Editor Plus. The design was input into the computer from the original hand cross stitch charts—one cross at a time. Be sure to follow the copyright laws as it may be illegal to scan a hand cross stitch chart into software. Many hours were spent creating each cross while following the original chart. The final design was then opened in the editing program and cut into sections that could be stitched in a large hoop. While in the editing program, alignment stitches were inserted to assist in aligning the sections. With the aid of a material setter for accurate alignment, the pieces were stitched to form one perfectly aligned design. It was stitched on 14 point cross stitch cloth using 13 colors of thread from black to a very pale gray.

A lways trim jump stitches before and after a color stop. Sometime it is even good to trim jump stitches during the embroidery of a single color that jumps from place to place in the hoop. This will assure a clean design that is crisp and looks hand embroidered.

*– Robert Decker*

# Robert Decker (continued)

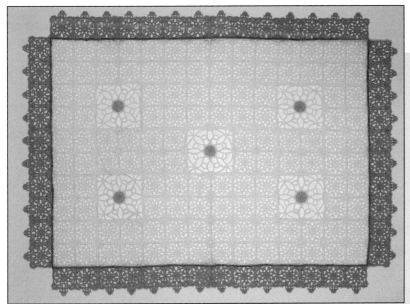

## Laced Elegance

Using the exquisite lace designs of Kae Barron's *K-Lace* from Criswell Embroidery & Design, this piece has a stitch count over 1 million. It is embroidered entirely from 100 percent cotton and 60-weight thread, both in the needle and the bobbin. The lace was embroidered entirely on a very heavyweight water-soluble stabilizer. The large square design was opened in the Husqvarna Viking Stitch Editor Plus and a color stop was inserted before and after the center circle so that the circle could be embroidered in a different thread color. The individual designs were opened in the Husqvarna Viking Customizing Plus where they were combined into embroiderable sections. After the sections were embroidered and before the removal of the water-soluble stabilizer, the sections were pieced together using a narrow, loose satin stitch. To give the piece additional stability after the border was attached, cotton gimp cord was satin stitched over the border attachment line. The gimp cord added extra strength to the foundation, as the cotton thread is very soft after the stabilizer is removed from the thread. After the assembly was completed, the piece was soaked for eight to 10 hours to completely dissolve the stabilizer from the lace.

## Pennsylvania Dutch Placemat and Napkin

The designs used for the placemat and napkin are from the Decker Design Studio— Pennsylvania Dutch 2nd Edition. To display the Pennsylvania Dutch designs, a set of dark blue ready-made placemat and napkin pieces were selected. The traditional colors in Dutch designs are always bright, using red, yellow, golden yellow, bright green and blues. The placemat was heavy enough that it was embroidered without any stabilizer. If you are embroidering on dark fabrics, consider using black bobbin thread. That way, you do not have to be concerned about the bobbin thread showing on the back of your piece. The napkin was embroidered using a heavy water-soluble stabilizer.

# Embroideryarts

Richards Jarden, owner of Embroideryarts, specializes in the digitizing of monograms. Here's a sampling of projects using his designs.

### Wool Jacket

This beautiful wool jacket features individual letters from the Embroideryarts Victorian Set 1 and a series of motifs from various monogram groups. The small motifs around the buttonholes are from the *Arabesque Monogram Set 2.* When monogramming, consider adding some interest to the letters by combining individual small motifs in embroidery customizing software on a computer. The jacket was created by Pauline Richards, editor of the *Total Embellishment Newsletter*.

### CD Case

This cleverly monogrammed CD case utilizes letters from the Embroideryarts *Arts & Crafts Monogram Set 3.* This easy project is a fun way to personalize a music CD or an embroidery design CD. A flower cluster motif was added to accentuate the monogram. To create the flower cluster in editing software, isolate the flower that is part of each left-side letter in the *Arts & Crafts Monogram Set 3.* Copy the element and paste two additional copies in the software. Then, save the flower as a new design with a new filename. To add a little extra interest, rotate two of the motifs as shown, slightly enlarged one flower and slightly reduce the other. Let your creativity be your guide.

*Photos courtesy of Embroideryarts.*

# Embroideryarts (continued)

### Terrycloth Towel

This monogrammed terrycloth towel utilizes designs from the Embroideryarts *Diamond Monogram Set 4* along with a specially digitized companion background design. Sewing monograms on terrycloth can be tricky because of all the loops in the toweling. The background design is a light density diamond-shaped fill pattern, digitized with a parallel stitch and a satin stitch border. The background design functions as a base for the monogram, controlling the loops, and provides a frame for the three-letter monogram. Embroider the background motif in a color of thread that matches the fabric for an attractive tonal effect.

### Napkin

This elegantly monogrammed napkin features two-letter monogram designs from the Embroideryarts *Diamond Monogram Set 2.* Use your favorite alignment tool to aid with the centering of the motifs directly above the decorative hemstitch. Hoop a piece of tear-away stabilizer, spray the stabilizer with temporary adhesive and secure the napkin to the stabilizer. This is the easiest way to embroider napkin corners.

### Basket

This museum-quality, Nantucket basket with a padded monogrammed top, utilizes letters from the Embroideryarts *Diamond Monogram Set 3.* This monogram style is the perfect complement for the 4" (102mm) diameter basket as the lettering background is a woven fill stitch to complement the basket features.

# Dana Bontrager

Dana is the owner of Purrfection Artistic Wearables and has made a career of "thinking outside the fashion box." She is continually stretching design and sewing conventions to develop new skills and creativity. Working from her studio in the Pacific Northwest, she designs Paw Prints Patterns and Pelle's See Thru Stamps™ to enable the wearable artist to create unique, eye-catching garments that are both casually simple and wonderfully imaginative.

## Swirl Jacket

Dana used the Purrfection Jakarta pattern made from twill and cotton to embroider the swirls with the Husqvarna Viking *Primitives* card #9. She rubber stamped swirls on the lining with Pelle's See Thru Stamps. Pieced elegance at its best!

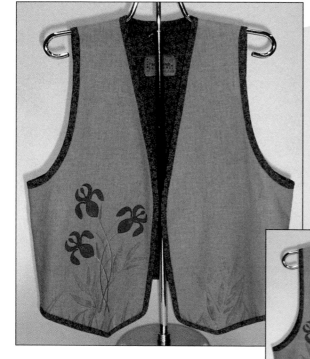

## Linen Iris Vest

Dana used the Purrfection Patchwork Vest as the canvas to embroider the stems with the Husqvarna Viking *Embroidery Sampler* card #100, to rubber stamp the iris flowers with Pelle's See Thru Stamps, and to stencil the eucalyptus leaves from the *ReVisions* collection. The combination of all three on linen and coordinating quilter's cotton makes the perfect fabric texturing and dimensional embellishment.

# Dana Bontrager (continued)

### Fleece Jacket

Dana used the Purrfection *Mosaic* pattern to create this luscious fleece jacket to embroider the stems with the Husqvarna Viking *Embroidery Sampler* card #100 and the letter "O" from the Husqvarna Viking *Kalligraphia Alphabet* card #100. The addition of color coordinating quilter's cotton as the trim makes the perfect accent with embroidery.

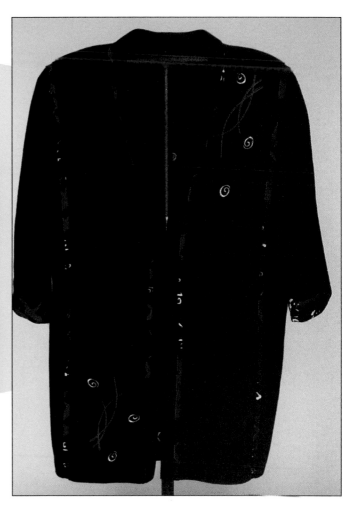

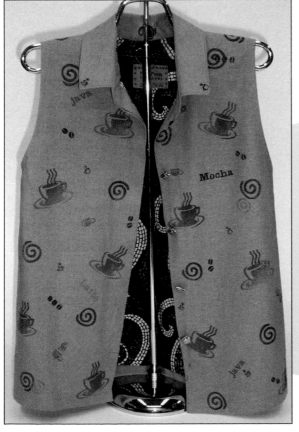

### Coffee Vest

Dana used the Purrfection *Sahara* pattern made from linen to embroider the coffee related text with the Husqvarna Viking *Clarendon Alphabet* card #100, to rubber stamp the coffee stamps with the Pelle's See Thru Stamps, and to stencil the coffee beans from the *ReVisions* collection. This is the perfect vest for coffee lovers!

# Donna Vermillion Giampa

Award-winning designer, Donna Vermillion Giampa, has been widely known in the hand cross stitch arena for more than 20 years. In addition to the creation of hand cross stitch designs, Donna also digitizes designs for use on an embroidery machine. Donna is the owner of Vermillion Stitchery, specializing in elegant cross stitch designs and ornament sets in a wide variety of themes.

### Flower Babies Quilt

Frame your cross stitch embroidery designs with color coordinating cotton fabric for wall décor. These lovely *Flower Babies,* stitched on a linen-cotton blend fabric, are surrounded by an assortment of 100 percent cotton fabrics pieced, then quilted, to enhance the playful babies. The *Flower Babies* designs are stitched with DMC 50-weight cotton machine embroidery thread, and are available from The Vermillion Stitchery.

### Toddlers & Toys Door Hangar

This little stuffed pillow for your baby or small child's room features the *3 Toddlers* design stitched on a linen-cotton blend fabric using DMC 50-weight machine embroidery thread. The precious children are surrounded by a striped 100 percent cotton fabric border and pink ruffle, all tied up with a tiny satin bow and hanging ribbon.

# Donna Vermillion Giampa (continued)

### Patriotic Santa Banner

The Vermillion Stitchery's *Nine Santas* collection is showcased in this patriotic banner, stitched on blue 100 percent cotton fabric using the same threads as featured above. The three Santas are surrounded by a series of four pieced borders, using various 100 percent cotton prints in red, white and blue. A metallic gold cord with tassels sets off the gold threads used in the Santas.

### Chimney Santa

This lovely, old-fashioned Santa is stitched on a linen-cotton blend fabric using DMC 50-weight cotton machine embroidery thread. The design, framed with a tiny red border and holly-print fabric outer border, is included in the *Classic Santas* collection from The Vermillion Stitchery.

### Nine Santas Quilt

Donna Giampa's *Timeless Santas* are featured in a wall quilt showcasing all nine designs. The 3" designs are stitched on a linen-cotton blend fabric with DMC 50-weight cotton machine embroidery thread and gold metallic thread. A mixture of 100 percent cotton prints and plaids create an additional design to showcase the Santas.

# Embroidery Design and Graphic Image Formats

Here is a listing of embroidery design and graphic image formats. These three-letter extensions represent a file format type that can be opened by embroidery or graphic art software. Not all software packages can open every file format. Get to know the file formats your embroidery or graphic art software can open, import, or export. For more information on the formats your software can utilize, consult your embroidery software manual, the software manufacturer's Web site, or the place of purchase.

## Embroidery Design File Formats

| Format | Embroidery Machine Manufacturer/Software Manufacturer |
|---|---|
| 10o | Toyota (Commercial) |
| ART | Bernina |
| ASD | Melco (Commercial) |
| CND | Melco Condensed (Commercial) |
| CSD | POEM, Singer EU, Viking Huskygram |
| DST | Tajima (Commercial) |
| EMB | Wilcom (Commercial) |
| EMD | Elna (Exquisite), Singer (XL-5000) |
| EXP | Melco Expanded (Commercial) |
| FDR | Barudan (Commercial) |
| FMC | Barudan (Commercial) |
| GNC | GN Scalable (Great Notions) |
| HUS | Husqvarna Viking/Pfaff (2140) |
| JEF | Janome (10000) |
| KSM | Pfaff (Commercial) |
| OEF | OESD |
| OFM | OESD |
| PCD | Pfaff |
| PCM | Pfaff – MAC |

| Format | Embroidery Machine Manufacturer/Software Manufacturer |
| --- | --- |
| PCQ | Pfaff |
| PCS | Pfaff – Windows (7570 and earlier models) |
| PEC | Baby Lock, Bernina (Deco), Brother, Simplicity, White |
| PES | Baby Lock, Bernina (Deco), Brother, Simplicity, White |
| PHC | Baby Lock (Ellageo), Brother (2000 series) |
| PSF | Pulse software (Commercial) |
| PSW | Singer |
| SEW | Elna (CE20 and earlier models), Janome (9000 and earlier models), Kenmore |
| SHV | Husqvarna Viking (Designer 1, 2) |
| TAP | Happy (Commercial) |
| VIP | Husqvarna Viking (Designer 1, 2), Pfaff (2140) |
| XXX | Singer XL, Compucon (Commercial) |

# Graphic Art File Formats

| Format | File Type | File Description |
| --- | --- | --- |
| AI | Vector | Adobe Illustrator |
| BMP | Bitmap | Bitmap |
| CDR | Vector | Corel Draw |
| CGM | Vector/Bitmap | Computer Graphics Metafile |
| DXF | Vector | Autodesk Drawing eXchange Format |
| EMF | Vector/Bitmap | Windows Enhanced Metafile |
| EPS | Vector/Bitmap | Encapsulated PostScript |
| GIF | Bitmap | Graphic Interchange Format |
| J2K | Bitmap | JPEG2000 |
| JPG | Bitmap | Joint Photographic Experts Group |
| PCD | Bitmap | Kodak Photo CD |
| PCX | Bitmap | Zsoft Paintbrush |
| PNG | Bitmap | Portable Network Graphic |
| PSD | Bitmap | Adobe Photoshop |
| TIF | Bitmap | Tagged Image File Format |
| WMF | Vector/Bitmap | Windows Metafile |
| WPG | Vector/Bitmap | WordPerfect Graphics Metafile |

# Appendix II

# Design Organization Categories

Here are some category ideas that can be used to create an organization system on your computer. Study the example file path in the box below. Save designs under one main folder called "Embroidery." From this main folder, create sub-folders to catagorize designs. Refer to page 70 for more information on organizing designs.

## An example file path:

To find a "koala bear" design that you may have saved on your computer, follow this path:

**C:/embroidery/designs/individual designs/animals/bears/koala**

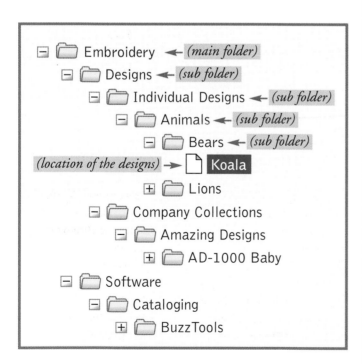

Refer to page 70 for more information on organizing designs.

---·--- **Individual Design Categories** ---·---

Alphabets
  Child
  Floral
  Fancy
Angels
  Cherubs
  Christmas
  Guardian
Animals
  Bears
  Lions
  Zebras
Appliqué
  Animals
  Gardening
  Geometric
Astrology
  Capricorn
  Pisces
  Sagittarius
Birds
  Eagles
  Robins
  State
Borders
  Corners
  Eyelet
  Geometric
Buildings
  Barns
  Houses
  Skylines
Business
  Awards
  Office Equipment
  Ribbons
Cartoons
  Clowns
  Faces
  Insects

Children
  Baby
  School
  Teens
Collections
  Antiques
  Stuffed Animals
  Sewing Machines
Country
  Barnyard Animals
  Roosters
  Tractors
Crafts
  Beading
  Painting
  Scrapbooking
Cutwork
  Borders
  Elegant
  Geometric
Elegant
  Holiday
  Large Designs
  Table Dressing
Fairies
  Fanciful
  Tooth
  Whimsical
Fall
  Apples
  Leaves
  Trees
Fashion
  Allover Designs
  Buttonhole Designs
  Shoes
Favorites
  Combined Designs
  Edited Designs
  Holiday or Gift Giving

Flags
   Foreign
   Nautical
   State or USA
Floral
   Bouquets
   Pansies
   Plants
Food
   Fruit
   Picnic
   Vegetables
Frames
   Basic Shapes
   Borders
   Picture
Fun
   Cartoons
   Humorous
   Unique
Games
   Cards or Dice
   Slot Machines
   Tic Tac Toe
Gardening
   Herbs
   Seed Packets
   Tools
Geometric
   Basic Shapes
   Retro
   Squiggles
Holidays
   Christmas
   Thanksgiving
   Valentines Day
House
   Country
   Kitchen
   Colonial
Insects
   Ants
   Beetles
   Cartoon
Lace
   Battenberg
   Fancy
   Stand Alone
Lighthouses
   Maine
   Michigan
   New England

Magazines
   Creative Machine
      Embroidery
   Designs in Machine
      Embroidery
   Sew News
Miniatures
   Floral
   Toys
   Transportation
Monograms
   Basic
   Fancy
   Floral
Music
   Instruments
   Musical Notes
   Piano
Nature
   Leaves
   Mountains
   Sun
Occupations
   Fireman
   Nurse
   Teacher
Ocean
   Shells
   Tropical Fish
   Whales
Outer Space
   Aliens
   Stars
   Planets
Outline
   Blackwork
   Bluework
   Redwork
Party
   Birthday
   Graduation
   Wedding
People
   Cartoons
   Family
   Stick Figures
Pocket Toppers
   Animals
   Sewing
   Tools
Quilting
   Outline Designs

Quilt Blocks
Thimbles
Recreation
   Hunting
   Fishing
   Golf
Religious
   Crosses
   Guardian Angels
   Churches
Sayings
   School
   Religious
   Humorous
School
   Books
   Bus
   Chalkboard
Sewing
   Machines
   Buttons or Snaps
   Seam Ripper
Shapes
   Circles
   Ovals
   Triangles
Sports
   Basketball
   Softball
   Volleyball

Spring
   Flowers
   Grass
   Rain
Summer
   Beach
   Picnic
   Sun
Tools
   Hammer
   Screwdriver
   Saw
Toys
   Dolls
   Rocking Horses
   Trains
Transportation
   Cars
   Trains
   Trucks
Winter
   Snowflakes
   Snowmen
   Ice Skating
World
   Flags
   Globes
   Ships

------- **Company Design Packs** -------

Amazing Designs
Baby Lock
Bernina
Brother
Sue Box
Cactus Punch
Criswell Embroidery
Dakota Collectibles
Dalco Home Sew
Decker Designs
Elna
Embroideryarts
Embroidery Central

Embroidery Machine
   Essentials
Suzanne Hinshaw
Janome
Kenmore
OESD
Pfaff
Martha Pullen
Simplicity
Singer
Sudberry House
Vermillion Stitchery
Viking
Zundt Designs

# Appendix III

# Playing With Words — Lettering Inspiration

Here is a fun list of sayings that can be used alone or combined with embroidery designs. The addition of words in embroidery is a fun way to express your creativity and give individual designs some pizzazz.

Use customizing or lettering software to form words in a multitude of font styles available. The designs provided with this book can be used to perfect your lettering skills. No matter the season, lettering can add humor, heartfelt meaning, or visual expression to embroidery.

The designs featured on pages 116-120 are from the CD-ROM, Cactus Punch, Dakota Collectibles and The Embroidery Resource.

## Aging

- Aged to Perfection!
- Forget the hot flashes… give me some power surges!
- Growing old is inevitable… growing up is optional!
- I'd rather be 50 than pregnant!
- I'm not 40 — I'm 18 with some extra years of experience!
- I'm not aging…I just need re-potting!

- It's never too late to have a happy childhood!
- Old enough to know better… too old to care!
- Recycled Teenager
- We're retired…our job is to have fun!
- Wrinkles aren't so bad…they just show where smiles have been!
- Youth and Agility is no match for Age and Treachery!

I'm not old, I just need…

REPOTTING!

## Angel

- Never drive faster than angels can fly!
- Angels sent from heaven above, please protect the ones we love.

- Earthly angels are mothers in disguise.
- When in doubt…wing it!

Angels
sent from heaven above,
please protect
the ones we love.

## Babies, Kids and Parents

### For a Baby's Bib

- Finger food expert!
- I will smile for food!
- Lunch is on me!
- Oops!
- Under this mess is one really cute baby!
- WARNING: I drool at a moment's notice!

### For a Boy

- A chip off the old block!
  (Dad: The old block!)

### For Any Baby

- Babies are such a nice way to start people!
- Babies Rule!
- I give wet kisses!
- With this smile I can get away with ANYTHING!
- You mean you're supposed to sleep when it's dark?

Babies are such a nice way to start people!

## *Babies, Kids and Parents (continued)*

### For a Baby's Room Door

- Just see what happens if you wake the sleeping giant!
- Shhh…
- Sleeping Beauty

### Teen

- Whatever…
- Wild Thing!

### Toddler

- 2 cute 4 words!
- Please be patient…I'm a work in progress!

### Tween Girl

- Best (friend #1) Friends (friend #2) Forever (friend #3)
- Princess
- You Go Girl!

### Parents

- Be kind, I have a teenager!
- Discover wildlife… have kids!
- Parenthood is an heir raising experience!
- The best thing to spend on your children is TIME!
- We can handle any problem… we have kids!

The best thing to spend on your children is TIME!

## *Family and Friends*

### Friendship

- Friendship is our thread in the patchwork of life.
- Our friendship is like a cup of coffee… a special blend of you and me!

### Grandparents

- Grandmas are just antique little girls!
- Grandpas are just antique little boys!

### Men

- Home of the Lawn Ranger!
- I refuse to grow up!
- Still plays with cars!
- Tool Tycoon!

### Mom

- "M" is for mother…not maid!
- A mother holds her children's hands for a while… their hearts forever.
- Ask not what your Mother can do for you… ask what you can do for your Mother!
- Every mother needs a maid!
- MOM is WOW upside down!
- Motherhood is not for wimps!
- Motherhood: God's highest calling
- Queen Bee!

### Women

- WARNING: I have PMS and I'm all out of Chocolate!

*Friendship is our thread in the patchwork of life.*

MOTHERHOOD
God's Highest Calling

## *Food*

- Chocolate is an essential nutrient!
- Dressed to Grill!

- If you want breakfast in bed… sleep in the kitchen!
- Enjoy life – it's delicious!

Enjoy Life!

*it's delicious*

## Gardening

- Flower Power!
- Have a Bloomin' Good Day!
- In my garden, love grows!
- Love grows here!
- Nurture Nature!
- Plant Manager
- She who has flowers in her garden has flowers in her heart.

LOVE
*grows here*

## Home

- A bachelor lives here…enter at your own risk!
- A man is the King of his castle until the Queen comes home!
- Bless this mess!
- Dust is a protective cover for our furniture!
- Home is where you hang your heart.
- Our guests make us happy…some coming in… and some going out!
- The home of a Domestic Engineer.
- There's no place like home.
- Welcome to Grand Central Station.

*There's no place like*

H·O·M·E

## Holidays

### Christmas

- CHRIST is the best part of CHRISTmas!
- Christmas is for sharing and caring.
- Dear Santa, I want it ALL!
- Define "naughty"…
- HO, HO, HO!
- It's too late to be good!
- Just say HO!
- Love was born on Christmas morning!

### Kid's Christmas

- Dear Santa… I can explain!
- Show me the presents!
- Twinkle, Twinkle Little Star

### Pet's Christmas

- Santa Paws

### Halloween

- Too Cute to Spook!
- Coffin Break!
- Home of the wicked witch and all her little spiders!
- Bat Mom

### Graduation

- The tassel is worth the hassle!

Just Say…
HO!

*Christmas is for sharing and caring*

## Life

- Blessed are they who can laugh at themselves for they shall never cease to be amused!
- Experience is the best teacher… but the tuition is costly!
- For every problem there's an opportunity!
- Go ahead…take my advice… I'm not using it anyway!
- I don't do mornings!
- I used to have a handle on life… until it broke.
- If it weren't for the last minute, nothing would get done!
- Is it coffee yet?
- It's never the wrong time to do the right thing.
- Life is Too Important to Take Seriously
- Marriages are made in heaven… so are thunder and lightning!

Is it
COFFEE
yet?

## *Life (continued)*

- Of all the things I've lost… I miss my mind the most!
- Okay, who stopped payment on my reality check?
- Smile!
- Stressed spelled backwards… DESSERTS!
- Too much of a good thing is WONDERFUL!

- When in doubt, look up!
- With enough coffee anything is possible!
- A smile adds to one's face value!
- Catch a smile!

## *Pets and Animals*

### Bear
- Friends make everything bearable!
- Grin & Bear It!
- Stuffed with Love
- You are Beary Special!

### Bird
- Home Tweet Home
- Winter is for the birds!
- Talk birdie to me!

### Cat
- "MEW" spoken here!
- Cats understand the importance of naps!
- Dogs have owners… cats have staff!
- I'm not rude…I've got cat-i-tude!
- Tiger in training!
- Princess

### Cow
- Got Cookies?
- Have you herd the moos?

### Dog
- Beast
- My dog isn't spoiled, I'm just well trained!
- The Welcome Waggin'!

### Frog
- So many frogs…so few princes!
- Toadally Hoppy!

### Pets
- I may not be perfect, but my dog thinks I am!

### Rabbit
- Hop to it!
- Somebunny Loves You!

### Sheep
- Bless Ewe!
- Ewe are my sunshine!
- There's only one ewe!
- It's ewe and me forever!

**You are BEARY Special!**

**MEW SPOKEN HERE**

**Home Tweet Home**

## *Quilting*

- A quilt is something you make to keep someone you love warm!
- Blessed are the children of the piecemakers…for they shall inherit the quilts!
- Life is a patchwork of FRIENDS!
- Quilt 'til you wilt!
- Quilters form the stitches that hold the world together.

- Quilting with friends will keep you in stitches!
- Quilts are like friends… a great source of comfort!
- Those who sleep under a quilt sleep under a blanket of love.
- When life gives you scraps… make a quilt!
- Sewing and Quilting fill my days…not to mention the kitchen, bedroom and closets!

*Sewing and Quilting fill my days… not to mention the kitchen, bedroom and closets!*

## Sewing

- Born to Sew, Forced to Work!
- Creative minds think alike!
- Don't put all of your spools in one basket!
- I don't have a fabric stash… I have a collection!
- If I sew fast enough, does it count as an aerobic exercise?
- Life's a Stitch!
- One who sews wears their threads.

- One yard of fabric, like one cookie, is never enough!
- Sew much fabric…sew little time!
- Sewing mends the soul.
- Sewing with friends will keep you in stitches!
- Stitch your stress away!
- You're SEW special!

## Sports

- Sweat + Endurance = Success

### Fishing

- An old fisherman and the catch of his life live here!
- Born to Fish, Forced to Work!
- Women Want Me, Fish Fear Me!

### Golf

- Born to Golf, Forced to Work!
- I can still drive 300 yards…in my golf cart!
- I'm not over the hill…just on the back nine!

### Baseball

- It isn't just a bat…it's a launching pad!

## Teacher

- Kids are my business!
- Teachers plant the seeds of the future
- Teachers touch the future!

- The art of teaching is the art of assisting in discovery.
- You can't scare me… I teach!

## Winter

### Snow

- Let it snow! Let it snow! Let it snow…someplace else!
- Snowmen fall from the sky unassembled.
- There's no people like SNOWPEOPLE!

### Mittens

- Hi/Bye (on underside)
- Right/Left (on top)